A History of Development Economics Thought

This book explores the history of economic development thought, with an emphasis on alternative approaches in macro development economics.

Given that the pioneers of development economics in the 1940s and 1950s drew inspiration from classical political economists, this book opens with a review of key classical scholars who wrote about the progress of the wealth of nations. In reviewing the thinking of the pioneers and those that followed, both their theories of development and underdevelopment are discussed. Overall, the book charts the evolution of development economic thought from the early developmentalists and structuralists, through to the neo-Marxist approach and radical development theory, the neo-liberal counter revolution, and the debate between new developmentalists and neo-liberal scholars. It ends with an assessment of the state of the field today.

This book will be of interest to all scholars and students interested in the evolution of development economics.

Shahrukh Rafi Khan is Visiting Professor of Economics at Mount Holyoke College, USA.

Routledge studies in development economics

A History of Development Economics Thought

Challenges and counter-challenges

Shahrukh Rafi Khan

Routledge
Taylor & Francis Group

LONDON AND NEW YORK

First published 2014 by Routledge

2 Park Square, Milton Park, Abingdon, Oxfordshire OX14 4RN
52 Vanderbilt Avenue, New York, NY 10017

Routledge is an imprint of the Taylor & Francis Group, an informa business

First issued in paperback 2019

British Library Cataloguing in Publication Data
A catalogue record for this book is available from the British Library.

Library of Congress Cataloging in Publication Data
Khan, Shahrukh Rafi.
  A history of development economics thought : alternative approaches /
Shahrukh Rafi Khan.
  pages cm. – (Routledge studies in development economics)
  Includes bibliographical references and index.
  1. Economic development–History. 2. Economics–History. I. Title.
  HD82.K436 2014
  338.9001–dc23
                                                        2013033407

ISBN: 978-0-415-67630-4 (hbk)
ISBN: 978-0-367-86649-5 (pbk)

Typeset in Times New Roman
by Wearset Ltd, Boldon, Tyne and Wear

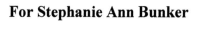
For Stephanie Ann Bunker

Contents

xiv *Contents*

PART IV
Neo-liberalism challenged 107

Acknowledgments

Thanks are due to the three anonymous reviewers of this book's proposal for their thoughtful comments and suggestions. I am particularly grateful to my editor, Robert Langham, for his excellent comments and guidance in the initial stages of the book's conception and for having faith in my ability to tackle what for me was a very ambitious project. Thanks also to Natalie Tomlinson of Taylor & Francis for her patience and responsiveness and also for her gently but firmly setting deadlines and then sending reminders. Chelsea Wurms text edited the manuscript and in this regard went way beyond the call of duty in making excellent comments to enhance clarity and consistency. I thank Mount Holyoke College for financial support and for being a great place to work.

Preface

"there is nothing new under the sun"
Ecclesiastes 1:9

The quote above comes to mind when reflecting on the history of thought in the field of macro development economics, starting, as one must, with classical scholars and the development economic pioneers. There have been many refinements, much formalization, and improved measurement. But if current development economists bothered to read the classics and the pioneers, they might find many of their own ideas reflected in what has already been said.[1] Similarly, it might be found that many of the criticisms of these pioneers were misplaced.

Conventional development economics textbooks are organized by topic. This topical organization does not reflect how thinking in the field has evolved. It also does not do justice to the topical linkages or the important debates in the subject. This book adopts a history of economic development thought approach with an emphasis on alternative approaches in macro development economics. This format, which follows the evolving debate in the discipline, is more lively and interesting and also I think more true to the spirit of the subject. This book is designed to complement textbooks in development economics but can also be a standalone monograph for scholars and students interested in the evolution of macro development economics.

Because the pioneers of development economics in the 1940s and 1950s drew on classical political economists, this book starts with a review of key classical scholars who wrote about the progress of wealth of nations.[2] Marx is included because, while his work was mostly focused on the critique of political economy and capitalism, his writings inspired the radical strain in development economics thought. The review of Marx, like the review of classical scholars in general, is thus selective. It focuses on presenting ideas that inspired later thinkers on colonialism and imperialism.

While there are many contributors to macro development economics thought, in the interests of brevity the focus is on key thinkers who made seminal contributions. In selecting authors to include I have tried to follow the broad consensus, but there are always differences of opinion.[3] Like all economists, I have biases and hence am among those who doubt that values can be suspended when doing social science. These biases must inevitably come into play in a book of this nature since it requires a reduction of hundreds and even thousands of pages into a brief and coherent narrative.

Many important refinements and nuances by other authors are not pursued though they are generally mentioned. In addition, most of the writers whose contributions *are* reviewed are/were very prolific, so this review focuses on work that represented the breakthrough in thinking that brought them acclaim. One commonality among the writers reviewed is their prescience: their scholarship has demonstrated an uncanny ability to remain relevant long into the future. It is this remarkable aspect of these scholars' thinking that this book in particular focuses on.

Critiques by other scholars are generally not pursued, though references are generally provided, and so I am assuming the reader has basic knowledge of development economics and can be the judge. I avoid critically engaging with the arguments in the text and this too I have left to the reader. Comments are provided in the endnotes, or in the summary section, when I think they may be relevant.

I also have not pursued the polemics, particularly of the heterodox development economists. Mainstream development economists seem mostly oblivious or only vaguely familiar with the thinking of heterodox economists. Perhaps they do not care to engage with heterodox thinking because the mainstream appears to be overwhelming in numbers, even in low income countries, and partly it may be the vast difference in method.[4] In any case, if I had pursued the polemics mainstream economists would be struck (perhaps comforted) by how intently heterodox economists demolish each other's arguments and evidence. I take this to be a sign of a vibrant debate and not a cultural trait.

The terms used for the countries that the subject of development economics pertains to have changed over time starting from "barbaric," "primitive," and "backward" used by the classical scholars to "underdeveloped" and "developing" used by the pioneers of development economics. My preference is for the neutral terms "low income countries" (LICs), "middle income countries" (MICs), and "high income countries" (HICs) used by Nurkse (1967, p. 63) in the early 1950s. By referring explicitly to income, these terms focus on the trait that is of greatest interest for economic growth and development, while avoiding broader connotations that may not be accurate for all countries in a given income category. While I try to maintain Nurkse's usage when possible, the other terms are also used in certain contexts, particularly when referring to the ideas of certain scholars.

While classical scholars used the term "progress," the pioneers referred to "development," although both terms referred to economic growth. Even though both groups of scholars strongly recommended investing in health and education, they did so to make individuals more productive as inputs into the economic growth process. It was later heterodox scholars who distinguished the concept of development from that of economic growth. I use the two terms interchangeably until the discussion of development by these heterodox scholars in Chapter 5.

In reviewing the thinking of the pioneers and those that followed, both their theories of underdevelopment and theories of development are discussed. When the author's focus is disproportionately on one or the other, this is indicated. In each case, whether the proximate causes of development or underdevelopment are internal or external is identified and this fourfold classification is the simple conceptual schema pursued in the book. While some of the pioneers distinguished their work by critiquing that of other prominent scholars, this book focuses primarily on each author's original contribution in terms of a theory of development or underdevelopment as indicated earlier.

The chapter outline indicates none on institutional development economics and this may appear to be an omission. This is deliberate; in fact, most development economists are institutional economists, dealing as they do with markets and states and with the influence of policy on prices and wellbeing. Although some, like Gunnar Myrdal and Douglass North, are more self-consciously institutional, the focus on institutions is another commonality among all the scholars reviewed in this book.

"Mainstream" in this book refers to the economic philosophy of classical scholars that transformed after the marginal revolution into neo-classical economics. The challengers of the mainstream typically justify interventions to support, alter, or suspend the market mechanism because of a conviction about market failures or unjust market outcomes.

This book most closely follows the paths pursued by Hunt (1989) and Meier (2005). Invariably, preferences influence approaches to the subject matter and hence the terrain covered. More important, this book does not purport to be a comprehensive history of macro development economics theories or thought but focuses on key thinkers and their contributions and in some cases key debates.

In reviewing the literature, I found that there was often a lack of critical self-assessment. For example when exploring a debate on a particular issue, mainstream economists often assume that the "other" in these debates is driven by ideology, while maintaining that they themselves are rational, scientific and pragmatic. For example, Meier (2005, p. 89), who is among the leading documenters of development economics thought, recommends that ideas should "—avoid the biases of ideology" and as an example dismisses the concept of "center-periphery" (see Chapter 3) as emotive rather than logical. In fact, this view could be considered as ideological as the one dismissed since no explanation is provided about why the concept in question is emotive rather than logical.

Celso Furtado, a prominent Brazilian economist (see Chapter 4), suggested that "Possibly no concept has had so much significance for the advance of studies on development as Raul Prebish's concept of center-periphery structure" and goes on to explain why. Prebish was modest and suggests that no one has a monopoly on the truth that can at best only be glimpsed. He also argues for "—discarding dogmas and preconceived ideas, until we reach a measure of common ground."[5]

In the great debate about the degree of state intervention in the economy—a debate that finds particularly urgent expression in development economics—I side with those who push for public policy to promote social justice (defined following Myrdal (1957, p. 9) as more equality of opportunity).[6] However, this book is not about taking issue but about trying to faithfully give expression to the thought of the great economists who shaped the field. As stated earlier, occasionally endnotes are used for observations viewed as pertinent.

While I have been a student of development economics since the early 1970s, it has been a privilege to take the time to go back to studying the foundational contributions. The most humbling aspect of this process was discovering that the thinking of the classical scholars and development economics pioneers was so much broader and deeper than what I had previously imagined. Most pleasurable for me in writing this book as a process of discovery were the surprises and the nuggets of wisdom.

Notes

1 I co-edited a book after the 2007–2009 financial and economic crisis and suggested "market as means rather than master" as a sub-title after several searches to make sure it had not been used before. I found the exact phrase used by Myrdal (1957, p. 80) in a similar context when conducting research for this book. I expect that specialists in the history of economic thought would be able to trace the lineage of ideas I have attributed to the pioneers to earlier scholars.
2 Refer to ed. Meier (1994) on the influence of classical economics on development economics thought.
3 For an alternative selection of pioneers, refer to Jumo (2005).
4 Exploring the actual numbers in scholar orientation across the different continents and the associated causal speculations for these differences would make interesting reading.
5 The Furtado and Prebish quotes are drawn from Kay (1989), p. 9 and p. 1 respectively.
6 Another great related debate has been on whether industry or agriculture should be privileged. The two debates are related because "non-interventionists" object to the industrial policy measures adopted by the state to promote industry. However, the measures recommended to promote agriculture are often equally interventionist. These issues are discussed in Chapters 6 and 7.

References

Jumo, K. S. 2005. *The Pioneers of Development Economics: Great Economists on Development*. New Delhi/London: Tulika Books/Zed Books.
Hunt, D. 1989. *Economic Theories of Development: An Analysis of Competing Paradigms*. Savage, Maryland: Barnes & Noble Books.
Kay, C. 1989. *Latin American Theories of Development and Underdevelopment*. New York: Routledge.
Meier, G. M. 2005. *Biography of a Subject: An Evolution of Development Economics*. New York: Oxford University Press.

Meier, G. M. 1994. *From Classical Economics to Development Economics*. New York: St. Martin's Press.

Myrdal, G. 1957. *Economic Theory and Under-developed Regions*. London: Gerald Duckworth & Co., Ltd.

Nurkse, R. 1967. *Problems of Capital Formation in Underdeveloped Countries and Patterns of Trade and Development*. New York: Oxford University Press.

1   The classical and radical roots of development economics

Introduction

Modern microeconomics is focused primarily on the efficient allocation of resources, and its unit of analysis is the individual or the firm while modern macroeconomics is focused primarily on economic stabilization. By contrast, much of the work of classical political economists focused on the progress of the wealth of nations, its nature and causes, and the distribution of this wealth across classes. These issues remain relevant for low and middle income countries today (LICs/MICs) and so I start with the writings of key classical economists to learn their views on why and how nations progressed, one of the two main themes of this book.

Progress of nations is now thought of and referred to as "development," which addresses both the increase in the means of delivering wellbeing to a population, and the widespread realization of this wellbeing by the population. In addition to these theories of progress, a second theme in development economics pertains to theories of underdevelopment: why nations do not progress. Pertinent to this question are the many theories of colonialism and imperialism from which the heterodox strain of development economics emerged.

In addition to the direct relevance their theories still bear for LICs and MICs, one more reason to start with the classical economists is that they were well known to the pioneering development economists of the 1940s and 1950s, who often used the classical economists as a frame of reference.

Marx is included because, while his work was mostly focused on the critique of capitalism, his writings inspired the radical strain in development economics thought. The review of Marx, like the review of classical scholars in general, is selective. It focuses on presenting those ideas that inspired later thinkers on colonialism and imperialism. Marx's critique of classical economics and the capitalist system made class and distribution its centerpiece, and the new Marxist and political economic approaches in development economics also drew on this (see Chapter 3).

The reading of classical scholars and the narration of their views is focused, in this chapter, on tracing back the lineage of ideas and lessons that may continue to be relevant in contemporary development economics. The major classical economists pertaining to mainstream development economics thought are Adam Smith, Thomas Robert Malthus, David Ricardo and John Stuart Mill.[1] In the critical or radical school of thought, the ideas of Hodgskin, Marx, Hobson, Luxemburg, and Lenin are reviewed mainly with reference to theories of colonialism and imperialism that influenced heterodox development economics.

Mainstream classical political economy key thinkers on the progress of nations

Adam Smith (1723–1790)

Smith drew on prior thought, but was first to synthesize these ideas and present a systematic framework of an economy.[2] Smith's classic *The Wealth of Nations* (1908) contains five books. Book I is about the causes of the improvement in the productive powers of labor, the key to the prosperity of nations, and how wealth is distributed. Book II is about capital accumulation that entails continued prosperity. In Book III he distinguished between nations that focused on the industry of the country and those that focused on the industry of towns such as arts, manufacturing, and commerce. He contended that the latter lends itself to greater prosperity. In Book IV he reviewed the theories emanating from the policy focus on industry and in Book V he discussed state (sovereign)-society relations and public finance. I draw on portions of Books I–V as they pertain to explaining the prosperity or progress of nations.

Smith started Book I with reference to a "fund" (GDP) that is also referred to as the annual supply or revenue. He theorized that the size of the fund is determined principally by the skill and dexterity of the workforce and the judgment with which it is applied, and by the ratio of active and non-active labor (participation rate). These are central irrespective of other factors like the soil, climate and size of the nation. Smith noted that the division of labor and specialization contributed most to the productivity of the labor force and also distinguished advanced society from the more primitive ones. Because agriculture is by nature limited in the extent to which tasks can be sub-divided, labor productivity in manufacturing necessarily exceeds that in agriculture. Due to the greater potential for division of labor, and the ingenuity of machine makers whose inventions make tasks "easier and readier" (p. 8), time saving is also more likely in manufacturing

The stimulus for making labor more productive is thus the "propensity in human nature – to truck, barter and exchange one thing for another" (p. 10). The scope for such enhancing of labor productivity and producing a surplus for exchange is greater the greater the size of the internal market or access to a broader market via navigation.[3]

This broader social organization of production is addressed in chapter III of Book II. So far, we learn from Smith that nations progress due to skill and dexterity of the workforce, enhanced labor force participation rates and because higher labor productivity is induced by the division of labor and specialization.

Capital facilitates the latter via the invention of machines, which facilitate specialization and constrict the time needed for manufacturing processes. Accumulation thus occurs *prior* to the division of labor. Subsequent accumulation enables further specialization and prosperity rises proportionately. Capital circulates and transforms itself from money to goods for production and back into money and the circuit makes profit for the employers. For this to occur, nations need tolerable security, otherwise there is an incentive to bury capital for contingencies rather than consume it or employ it for profit (pp. 207–209).

The part of capital that is retained earns a profit and is referred to as fixed. This includes machines, trade instruments, land improvements, and human capital investments via education or apprenticeships. The other part circulates to pay for materials and wages and hence is not retained, but is parted with. Smith also distinguished between two types of labor. The [relative] progress of nations is determined by the part of labor that "adds value to the subject it is bestowed on" such as machinery and materials in manufacturing (p. 253). The other part of labor is not productive and perishes in the moment of performing a service. In this category Smith includes the sovereign and associated splendid court services, the ecclesiastic establishments and the military (p. 254), openly criticizing "great fleets and armies, who in time of peace produce nothing, and in time of war acquire nothing which can compensate for the expense of maintaining them, even while the war lasts." This criticism reflects Smith's belief that the prosperity of nations was dependent on a high ratio of productive to unproductive labor.

Smith argued that public prodigality (p. 263) can impoverish great nations by eating into the stock that can be used to hire productive labor. By the same token, nations could flourish as a result of the parsimony or frugality of individuals. Frugality is critical for increasing the fund that hires productive labor and it, rather than industry, is the immediate cause of the increase in capital (p. 260). Smith's optimistic evaluation was that in great nations, natural progress is maintained by frugality which offsets public extravagance. He asserted that the driving spirit behind this noble conduct was the "uniform, constant and uninterrupted effort of every man to better his condition" (p. 264). Since these motivations are universal, including in primitive societies, the other supportive conditions identified above such as the collective institutional framework must naturally come into play.

The great commerce of any civilized nation is carried on between town and country to the mutual benefit of both. Trade within a nation has the advantage of greater control over and security of capital, but the principle of mutual benefit from trade extends across borders (p. 290). Thus, if a nation can buy a good cheaper from another country, it should be done with some part of the produce of the country's industry (pp. 346–347).

The power of a country is always in proportion to the value of its annual produce and hence production is privileged (p. 287). Trade he clarifies is "—the symptom of great national wealth but it does not seem to be the natural cause of it" (p. 288). Thus, trade is principally an avenue for surplus. In serving this purpose it would also facilitate the process of capital accumulation. However,

Smith insisted that "Those statesmen, who have been disposed to favor it [trade] with encouragements, seem to have mistaken the effect and symptoms for the cause."

On balance he thought that colonies did add to the prosperity of nations with empires by opening up new markets and enabling additions to productive employment. However, this was despite the negative aspects of maintaining a monopoly on colonial trade, which created distortions in the flow of capital and hence reduced economic diversification (p. 473). In the case of dissension arising, Smith recommended a graceful exit. He believed that only foolish national pride and the personal interests of those administering the colonies, in conjunction with the interests of merchants, perpetuated an unprofitable course of [military] action (p. 480).

An element of Smith's theory of the state seemed to anticipate Marx. Smith wrote "Civil government, so far as it is instituted for the security of property, is in reality instituted for the defense of the rich against the poor, or of those who have some property against whose whom have none at all" (p. 560). Classical political economists following Smith quibbled or differed with him but all deferred to his genius in having established the framework and agenda for political economy.

Thomas Robert Malthus (1766–1834)

Malthus devoted Book II of his *Principles of Political Economy* (1951) to the progress of wealth. He viewed politics, security of property, and morals to be primary since without laws and good administration industry would be discouraged (p. 307). But Malthus thought these basic causes were likely to be satisfied in most civilized and prosperous countries, and so he focused on the proximate causes which allowed some countries to surpass others even when the basic causes were satisfied. This is the case even when some among these countries possessed fewer powers of production than others. So he focused his inquiry on "the most immediate and effective stimulants to the continued creation and progress of wealth" (p. 310).

In this regard, Malthus was concerned with countries that had already reached a certain threshold level of prosperity (improved) rather than with the primary causes of prosperity. As was the case with Smith, Malthus noted that structural change occurred when agriculture was very productive since this enabled a large section of the population to move to towns and into manufacturing (p. 335).[4] Structural change, along with demand from a growing middle class for "conveniences" and "luxuries," stimulated prosperity (p. 350).

By questioning Say's law of supply creating its own demand (p. 316), Malthus raised an issue that is still challenging for high income countries in a globalized world: the optimal level of national saving. Thus, Malthus did not support Say in ruling out a universal glut. While Ricardo accepted Say's law, arguing that since commodities are exchanged for commodities, and saving is lent and therefore consumed, overall effectual demand should remain constant even if the nature of expenditures may change. Malthus's rejoinder was that many commodities are exchanged for labor and it is relative to labor that they could lose value when there are market gluts. Since the same produce could command less labor "both the power of accumulation and the motive to accumulate would be strongly checked" (p. 317).

He also argued that the change in expenditure patterns that could accompany increased savings could be instrumental in producing a universal glut since asymmetries in production and effectual demand could result with regard to necessaries and luxuries. Malthus explained that this last point, which was accepted by Ricardo as merely a hypothetical possibility, was in fact the reality (p. 322).

Thus, while Malthus viewed parsimony to be a virtue, he pointed out that capital accumulation per se was not enough if "effectual demand" was lacking. He pointed out that it would be "equally vain" to raise capital accumulation without assured effectual demand as it would be to increase population without assured demand for labor (p. 330). He tried to establish this principle by exploring the reasons for the lack of effectual demand, and how it could explain the limited improvement in New Spain and Ireland as compared to England (pp. 331–351).

He summed up that the three great causes favorable to production were capital accumulation, labor saving inventions and soil fertility but in all cases the continued increase in wealth required adequate demand, domestic or foreign (p. 360). Subsequently, he approached policy analysis through this lens of effectual demand. For example, he advocated for better means of communication as a way to open up internal markets (pp. 361–362). He endorsed external trade as well, but echoed Smith in arguing that the reduction of import duties had to be selective and very gradual to avoid hurting domestic manufacturing (p. 428). Malthus also made a case for land distribution, based on his theory that the continued contribution to effective demand coming from a small number of large proprietors was limited in comparison to the demand generated by a moderate number who would be in "the middle ranks of life" (p. 374).[5]

Malthus attributed the rapidly growing wealth of the USA to the easy division of and access to land for the industrious and the contribution this made to effectual demand (p. 373). He reasoned that there must be an optimal land distribution since excessive redistribution could also hurt the accumulation process by not providing adequate demand for necessaries, conveniences, and luxuries emanating from the middle ranks of life (p. 376).[6]

Finally, Malthus made a case for taxation to fund expenditure on public works as a stimulus for consumption in certain periods, such as in the case of excess capacity following a war. He reasoned that capitalists saved out of their revenue and another body of consumers, not themselves engaged in direct production for the market, was needed (p. 398). He was cognizant that the benefit of public stimulus could be counter-balanced by the negative incentive effects of taxation, the accumulating interest on the national debt, and the negative impact on fixed income groups from the subsequent inclination to cheapen the currency via deficit financing (pp. 408–412).

David Ricardo (1772–1823)

Ricardo was a policy economist like his contemporary and friend Malthus. Ricardo's purpose, as stated in the original preface of his *Principles of Political Economy and Taxation* (1933), was to "determine the laws which regulate" the distribution of total produce into rent, profit, and wages. Because he, like Smith, believed that the wealth of nations was driven by capital accumulation, Ricardo was concerned with investigating factors that might arrest or stimulate the accumulation process. In this regard, he may have been the original "growth diagnostician."[7]

As he explained in the preface, central to his analysis was the explanation of what constitutes rent and he credited Malthus for having presented the true doctrine in 1815. The three agents in his analysis, claimants of rents, profits and wages, were landlords, capitalist farmers, and labor, respectively. Rents resulted from a scarcity of food relative to the needs of a population. Given variations in soil fertility, the most productive land, with its "original and indestructible powers of the soil" (p. 33), was able to command a premium over the less productive land, with the marginal land securing zero rent. In the situation of a new colony with an abundance of productive land, however, there would be no rent (p. 39). He assumed capital to be mobile and hence the returns to capital equalized across different activities and labor was given a subsistence wage (p. 36).

A cryptic statement on p. 40 attributed the increase in wealth across nations to three causes: "where disposable land is most fertile, where importation is least restricted, and where, through agricultural improvements, productions can be multiplied without any increase in the proportional quantity of labor, and where consequently the progress of rent is slow." In Ricardo's analysis, profits were a residual after paying subsistence wages and rent.[8] This explained why fertile land and agricultural imports were important. More fertile land would mean cheaper food and lower wages, and therefore higher profits. Food imports would have a similar effect in terms of lowering the price of food and thus the subsistence wage, and hence raising profits. In both cases, accumulation would be facilitated.

The third important factor that Ricardo referred to was agricultural improvements, and he considered two kinds (p. 42). One encompassed agricultural practices that affected all land in the same way, such as "more skilful rotation of crops or the better choice of manure." The other consisted of improvements that entailed a higher capital labor ratio, such as "improvements in agricultural implements, such as a plough and the thrashing machine, economy in the use of horses employed in husbandry, and a better knowledge of the veterinary arts" (p. 44).

With the former, the differential rent remained unchanged, although total rents could decline because the least productive land may no longer need to be used. If technological change affected land of different quality in different ways, rent would be affected. For example, if the least productive land were made more productive, rent would likely fall and vice versa but there would also be effects on the produce and hence wages to consider. Notwithstanding this nuance in analysis, the bottom-line for Ricardo was that rents and Corn Laws, which blocked cheap food imports, could be constraints on capital accumulation. This

Ricardian model essentially undergird Arthur Lewis's classic article in development economics reviewed in the next chapter.

John Stuart Mill (1806–1873)

Mill reviewed the laws governing the determination of key macro variables such as interest, profit, rents and wages, their inter-relationship and equilibrium in his *Principles of Political Economy* (1904). He dedicated Books I–III to a discussion of the current state of knowledge of these "statics," and turned in Book IV to "the dynamics of political economy" (p. 421). His focus, however, was not on the proximate causes of the progress of society per se, but rather on how social progress influenced production and distribution. He commented that the unlimited growth of "man's power over nature," the progress of science and technology, and the consequent ability to economize on labor while increasing its produce are part of the process of social progress (p. 422). He went on to document specific aspects of the development of civilized society that facilitated capital accumulation. Among these he included the continual increase in the security of persons and property and the increasing capacity for collective action or the "practice of co-operation" (p. 423). His general theory of the progress of society took account of capital accumulation, population growth, and improvements in the "productive arts" (science and technology).[9]

Like other classical political economists, Mill believed that growth would eventually cease when the end of the progressive state was succeeded by a stationary state. Mill himself had interesting speculations on a stationary society that reproduced itself in its current form. He denied the assumption of earlier political economists that the progressive state of society was preferable because the human condition in a stationary state would involve "trampling, crushing, elbowing and treading on each other's heels—" (p. 453). Mill suggested that the stationary state need not be unpleasant, especially because distribution policies could better the lives of the masses.

Mill recognized that science and technology and the outflow of surplus capital to "uncultivated or ill-cultivated regions of the earth" would allow society to push back the stationary state (p. 452), and accommodate more population, but he thought that improved nations had already attained adequate prosperity and that it was probably better for humans to avoid further progress to preserve nature and solitude (p. 454).[10] He recommended voluntary population control and suggested that the industrial arts should focus on enhancing leisure time.[11]

Radical classical political economy and theories of colonialism and imperialism: key thinkers

Thomas Hodgskin (1787–1869)

Hodgskin was a religious man who sought to make political economy consistent with the natural order. He took issue with Adam Smith and argued that the continued increase of the wealth of nations was the result of increased knowledge. He pointed out that inventions like the steam engine occur when the time is ripe, and that they require the cumulative increase in the knowledge of past generations. Population provided a positive stimulus and also the raw material for this accumulation of knowledge. Thus, his motto was: "Necessity is the mother of invention; and the continued existence of necessity can only be explained by the continual increase in people" (1966, p. 86).

Hodgskin recognized that, apart from increased knowledge and skill of society at large, capital accumulation could contribute to the wealth of nations. However, he qualified this by arguing that when a third party owns the capital, and "laborers must share their produce with unproductive idlers," then the progress of wealth would actually be retarded because "less of the annual produce is employed in reproduction." Furthermore, he noted that capital could only be made productive by the skillful hands of labor, and disputed the erroneous thinking of political economists who attributed productivity to dead machines, rather than to the skill and knowledge embodied in the labor that actually produced them (p. 252).

Hodgskin railed against the view that "lessening the reward to labor to add to the wealth of the idle can add to industry or accelerate the progress of society in wealth" (p. 254). On the contrary, weakening labor would only retard the increase in population and hence the stimulus to an increase in knowledge. He was not optimistic that the regulations on labor put into place by legislators were consistent with the natural order and therefore viewed them as impeding the progress of nations. "Social institutions which either will not allow the laborers to exert his productive power or rob him of its fruits" accounted for the increased poverty and social unrest of the times (p. 259).

Karl Marx (1818–1883)

Marx studied the relations of labor and capital more rigorously in order to develop his own theory of exploitation. As Avineri (1968, p. 4) observed, Marx's theory of economic development was the dialectical transformation of one mode of production into another. Marx's focus was on the analysis of capitalism, and he believed that the bourgeoisie, because of its immense productivity[12] and relentless search for new markets and raw materials, was the ultimate driver of globalization and "creates a world after its own image to facilitate capital accumulation" (Marx and Engels, 1988). The apparent "progress of nations" was merely part of the process whereby the capitalist world sowed the seeds of its own inevitable collapse.

The radical strain of development economics draws from Marx's theory of colonialism (Avinieri, 1968) and that is the focus of attention here.[13] The general problem was the collision between the capitalist regime in the mother country and self-employment in the colonies. Artisans and peasants enriching themselves were unlikely to be interested in enriching the capitalist needing to exploit wage workers for accumulation (p. 716). Quoting E. G. Wakefield, Marx agreed the solution was that "—dependence must be created by artificial means" (p. 721).

In America and Australia, the problem of creating dependence was exacerbated by the abundance of virgin land as public property was readily available for conversion to private property by those willing to start their own farms. This reduced the availability of labor and raised wages (p. 722). The solution was to put an artificial price on virgin soil making it relatively prohibitive for wage workers. At the same time, increased revenues from land sales funded the import of "have nothings" from Europe, who became wage workers for the capitalists. This was referred to as "systematic colonization" (p. 723).

By contrast, the problem encountered in the East was the lack of private property. In the introduction to his edited volume on *Marx on Colonialism and Modernization*, Avineri (1968, p. 6) observed that the absence of private property in the East was the basis of Marx's view that the Asiatic mode of production was stagnant with no internal motive for change.[14] It was subject to despotism with the state or sovereign as the ultimate owner demanding rent in kind. Village communities reproduced themselves (with the same name) as self-sufficient entities as their population expanded or if they were destroyed by natural disasters. Notwithstanding his acknowledgements of the horrors of colonialism, he viewed the destruction of these communities as a step forward since they led an "undignified, stagnatory, and vegetative life" and were oppressed by their own superstition, a caste system, rules, and a "brutalizing worship of nature" (pp. 88–89).

Thus, while Marx viewed the English to be driven "by the vilest interests, and stupid in the manner of enforcing them," they were instrumental in initiating a social revolution in stagnant societies (p. 89). By undermining spinning, weaving, and other handicrafts in India, British commerce tore apart the "unity of industrial and agricultural production," which Marx referred to in many newspaper essays on India (p. 44). The English he observed had a similar effect in China when, after wresting five ports by force, they flooded the markets with cheap machine-made goods that wiped out handicrafts.

Marx's assessment of the political economy of imperialism was that it was a mechanism to benefit some British subjects at tax-payers' expense. He wrote that the "advantage to Great Britain from her Indian Empire must be limited to the profits and benefits which accrue to individual British subjects. These profits and benefits, it must be confessed are very considerable" (1968, pp. 222–225). He went on in this essay to identify the beneficiaries who included stock-holders, recipients of patronage (civil, clerical, medical, military, and naval), and pensioners.[15] John Hobson, Rosa Luxemburg, and Vladimir Lenin elaborated on Marx's basic insights on colonialism.

John A. Hobson (1858–1940)

Hobson (1938, p. 4) distinguished colonialism from imperialism: He viewed colonialism as "migration of part of a nation to vacant and sparsely populated [temperate] lands, the emigrants carrying with them full rights of citizenship in the mother country." In this regard, it was the transplantation of national life abroad where "white colonists carry with them the modes of government, the industrial and other 'arts' of the civilization of the mother country" (p. 27). Imperialism, by contrast, meant dominating tropical and sub-tropical people and cultures by force for national advantage. The expected advantages included securing foreign markets for export, and facilitating the purchase of food and raw materials that could not be economically produced at home. In chapters 2 and 3, Hobson used statistics to affirm that trading, investing, and discharging surplus population were the real motives for imperial expansion. Echoing Marx, he argued that vested interests such as finance capital, which had much to gain from the imperial project, were able to put their own interests above those of the nation (pp. 48–49).

In terms of the political economy, the principal beneficiaries of imperialism were the investors seeking outlets for surplus capital (p. 51), along with the owners of the national debt (p. 108), the military industrial complex (including contractors, arms, and shipping manufacturers), and aristocrats seeking careers. Ultimately, these private profits were based on socialized risk since the state would become entangled if the foreign ventures met with obstacles (p. 56). Yet the press provided a patriotic spin for such ventures because they were owned or controlled by vested interests (p. 60).

However, for Hobson, this profit seeking was a manifestation rather than the root cause of imperialism. The root cause was the nature of the capitalist system in which capital accumulation and production outstripped consumption (p. 75). Growing protectionism in the advanced industrial nations compounded the problem (p. 77). He identified the underlying skewed distribution of income as the fundamental challenge to capitalism. Profits, rents, and interest secured much of the income for the rich while wages were restrained and not allowed to keep pace with productivity growth (pp. 82–83). Since the limited consumption of the rich was unable to provide the needed effective demand, capitalism sought alternative solutions. A supply side solution was combinations to limit production, which shut out the less competitive firms but this was only a partial solution (pp. 76–77). Demand side solutions included wasteful advertising (p. 85), but imperialism was the real solution. Therefore, as Hobson dug deeper, imperialism was ultimately the result of an unequal and unjust distribution of income and the civilized solution was social reform including welfare expenditures to ensure adequate effective demand.

Rosa Luxemburg (1871–1919)

Luxemburg (1951) accepted Marx's argument that capitalism needed non-capitalist social organizations in order to survive (p. 365). However, she took this concept further by pointing out that to go beyond simple reproduction within the Marxist framework, surplus value needs to be realized outside the sphere of capitalist production. Seeing that relations with the non-capitalist world were inevitable, she predicted that "capital, impelled to appropriate productive forces for purposes of exploitation, ransacks the whole world" (p. 358). Further, she pointed out that the "industrial reserve army of workers" would prove inadequate because, as Marx was aware, higher wages were not an adequate incentive to balance the propagation of population and labor with the pace of accumulation. Hence, she hypothesized that the "labor for this army is recruited from social reservoirs outside the dominion of capital." In particular, she suggested that "capital needs other races to exploit territories where the white man cannot work" (p. 361). Since labor power "is in most cases rigidly bound by the traditional pre-capitalist organization of production, – it must first be 'set free' in order to be enrolled in the active army of capital" (p. 362). So colonialism/imperialism was much more than simply a search for markets for surplus products; it was a much more broad-based need for the non-capitalist world to continue the accumulation process within the capitalist world.

Marx had maintained that self-sufficiency was anathema to capitalistic and imperialistic goals such as gaining possession of productive forces, coercing labor power into services, and separating industry from agriculture by destroying craft production, and Luxemburg provided detailed case studies of India, Algeria, and China in order to prove this point (chapter 29). She also conducted case studies of Egypt and Turkey to elaborate on the point that finance capitalism was another mechanism for subjugation of colonies because it provided unsustainable loans for dubious projects, and resulted in defaults, which then led to occupation (chapter 30).

Vladimir Lenin (1870–1924)

Lenin (1947) used statistics to demonstrate that Marx's prediction about the inevitable concentration of industrial capital had been realized in the early twentieth century via vertical integration, predatory pricing and other tactics (pp. 651–652). More important for Lenin was the fact that banking had also undergone a similar monopolization in the form of trusts, syndicates, and cartels (p. 655). Through interlocking directorships and the holding system, banks and finance capital acquired an immense amount of power over industry, commerce, services (p. 671), and every sphere of public life (p. 675). Surplus capital was exported to backward countries where capital was scarce and therefore expected to earn a higher return based on cheaper prices for land, materials and labor in particular (p. 688). Inter-imperialist conflict was inevitable in this search for profits as the whole non-capitalist world had been divided into zones of influence by the end of the nineteenth century and so only a redivision was possible. This conflict was exacerbated due to competition for increasingly scarcer raw materials (p. 704).

Summary and conclusions

While they differed in many important ways, all classical economists agreed that capital accumulation was central to the progress of the wealth of nations. Smith can be viewed as the first systematic and pragmatic economist concerned with the progress of nations (development). His prescription to focus on saving, capital accumulation and industry as catalysts for labor productivity growth still has resonance. In identifying human capital as part of fixed capital he pre-empted later mainstream theorists. He also anticipated Marx in his view of the role of the state. His very functional view of trade as an avenue for surplus and as a symptom rather than a cause of prosperity may also surprise mainstream theorists.

While Smith focused on the supply side and assumed demand would be present, Malthus worried about ensuring adequate effectual demand in order to maintain prosperity. An efficient agricultural sector was central to this process because it enabled rural urban migration, stimulated industry, and also created an urban middle class that sustained effective demand. While trade could con-tribute to effective demand by extending the market, Malthus echoed Smith in arguing that reciprocal trade liberalization should be approached with great caution to avoid hurting domestic industry. He was among the first economists to advocate land redistribution consistent with his broader goal of ensuring ade-quate effective demand. He reasoned that a few large proprietors would con-tribute less to effective demand than would a much larger number in the "middle ranks of life." However, he refrained from pushing this reform for other class based reasons.

Ricardo's focus was on potential hindrances and encouragements to capital accumulation and hence economic growth. To explore this issue, he developed a model based on the division of the total produce into rents, wages and profits. Wages were determined by subsistence, and profits were defined as a residual, so that elaborating on the theory of rents was central to his analysis. Any change that enhanced profits would enhance capital accumulation and growth. Profits could be enhanced by cheaper food, either via imports or via improvements in agricultural productivity. Technological change that applied across the board to soils of differ-ent fertility or made less productive land more productive could lower rents and raise profits. His theory of comparative advantage made the case for free trade (repeal of the Corn Laws) as being mutually beneficial for nations, but his under-lying concern was the need to sustain the accumulation process in Britain.

John Stuart Mill had a unique take on the growth process. Apart from the usual proximate causes, he viewed the progress of society as resulting from col-lective action or what he referred to as "a practice of cooperation." The right institutions, namely those that promoted security, science, and technology, were critical. He conceded that most political economists preferred economic growth (progressive state of society) to the stationary state, but that there were reasons to be careful about what one wished for. The progressive state inevitably pro-moted a rat-race and he suggested that most advanced countries had already attained adequate prosperity and should be focusing instead on redistributing wealth to ensure the welfare of the poor. Mill argued that science, technology, and colonialism were pushing back the stationary state, so nature and solitude needed to be preserved since these would inevitably be crushed by such eco-nomic growth. Also, he argued, science and technology should be harnessed to enrich the time spent in leisure.

The radical stream in the political economy of development can be traced back to Hodgskin (1966). He attributed the progress of nations to the accumulation of knowledge and skills. He argued that machines simply embodied the knowledge and skill of labor, and that attributing productivity growth to dead machines was misguided. Population growth stimulated the growth in knowledge by enhancing social needs, and knowledge rose to the occasion to meet these needs. Progress would be most effective when labor was able to retain the fruits of its effort rather than having to share it with idlers. But if profit was partly appropriated by idlers, the result would be lower labor remuneration, lower population growth and hence a lessened stimulus to the growth in knowledge.

Marx was able to more rigorously formalize the theory of exploitation that Hodgskin referred to. However, it was his theory of colonialism that is the root of radical development economics. He viewed the self-sufficiency of natural economies, which stemmed from the "unity of industrial and agricultural production," as being on a collision course with the global capitalist system. Since natural economies had no need for the industrial goods of capitalist economies, economic dependence had to be created via artificial means i.e. via the destruction of the natural economies. Hobson, Luxemburg, and Lenin elaborated on this basic insight.

Hobson distinguished between colonialism and imperialism. The former he viewed as the settlement of lands with temperate climates by whites who destroyed and displaced native populations and recreated the way of life of the mother countries. Imperialism was the forceful domination of alien peoples and cultures in tropical regions to ensure that imperialist countries had the supply of labor, materials, and markets needed for accumulation. The impetus for imperialism was created by wage repression and hence and unequal distribution of income and wealth in the imperialist countries, which resulted in a lack of effective demand and hence the search for foreign markets.

Luxemburg argued that the logic of accumulation in industrial countries required the realization of surplus value outside the sphere of capitalist production to go beyond simple reproduction. Thus, the drive to imperialism was based on more than simply a search for markets. She elaborated on the process by which imperialism subordinated natural economies in its drive for capital accumulation, using case studies of several countries including India, China, and Egypt.

Lenin used statistics to demonstrate that capital concentration had reached a zenith as a result of recurring crises, thus bearing out Marx's prediction. However, banks had also undergone a process of concentration via the formation of trusts, syndicates, and cartels and had acquired increasing power such that finance capital dominated other sectors of the economy like industry and commerce. Imperialism was a manifestation of the drive for profit by finance capital since the returns to capital in backward, capital-scarce nations was likely to be higher than in the capital-abundant industrialized economies.[16]

Notes

1 The marginal revolution ushered in by William Stanley Jevons, Carl Menger, Leon Walras and Alfred Marshall shifted the focus of attention from capital accumulation, production, and distribution to the micro issues of resource allocation and efficiency, i.e., away from the causes of the progress of wealth of nations.

2 Goodacre (2005, p. 27) concludes in his paper that the search for the roots of "today's development economics" lead back to William Petty.

3 There is a seeming disconnect in Smith's thinking here in that the propensity referred to is that of the individual but production is socially organized. Certainly individuals become more prosperous and contribute to prosperity by allowing themselves to fit into the division of labor and specialization of the vast impersonal economic system that they become part of. However, individuals do not organize production and in this sense the driving force for greater prosperity in the capitalist market system is also the collective institutional framework that enables production and the profit motive driving it, a framework Smith is well aware of.

4 This process is central to Arthur Lewis's model of rural-urban migration and structural change as will be explained in the next chapter.

5 For various reasons such land distribution was not recommended for England. The landed aristocracy was viewed as contributing to consumption, keeping the tyranny of the monarch in check (industrialists were concerned only with their own accumulation), and promoting the arts, and primogeniture induced other sons to serve productively in the professions or military.

6 This awareness of proportions is more broadly the case in Malthus's analysis such as in the optimal ratio unproductive to productive labor. He argues that these would vary according to circumstances such as the fertility of the soil, the progress of invention of machines, skills, and the degree (propensity) of consumption of different producers and tastes. He argued that precise determination was "beyond the resources of political economy." His cautionary note was "that the science of political economy bears a nearer resemblance to the science of morals and politics than to the science of mathematics" (p. 434).

7 Growth diagnostics is a tool of macro development economics designed to identify the key constraint(s) to economic growth (Hausmann, Rodrik, and Velasco, 2008).

8 Differential rent equalized the profit rate ($\rho = \Pi/W$) on farms of different fertility where Π is total profit and W real wages. Also, given capital mobility, the returns to capital would be equalized in agriculture and industry and this explained the crucial role of rents in Ricardo's analysis.

9 This is the starting point of modeling and measurement in neo-classical growth theory.

10 This notion of society having plenty and that the focus should be on redistribution was brought up much later in development economics by Sen (1982) in his exploration of famines.

11 Mill's prescient thought is consistent with modern day ecological economics, though policy makers and citizens in many low and low middle income countries would probably still view themselves as a long way from having attained adequate prosperity.

12 Avinieri quotes Marx: "[In] scarce one hundred years [the bourgeoisie], has created more massive and more colossal productive forces than have all preceding generations together."

13 For a broader view of Marx's influence on development refer to Sutcliffe (2008).

14 Luxemburg (1951, pp. 272–273) takes classical economists, particularly Mill, to task for this view regarding the absence of private property which she demonstrated to be erroneous.

15 South Asian scholars like Alam (2000) view the outflows from India to far exceed the inflows due to colonialism.

16 The ascendency of finance capital and its attempt to garner ever higher returns was noted again a century later by mainstream economists in 2007– 2008 as bubbles burst (housing, credit, stock) and a deep and extended economic crisis followed in the wake of the financial crisis in the USA, Europe, and other parts of the global economy.

References

Alam, M. S. 2000. *Poverty from the Wealth of Nations.* London: Macmillan.

Avineri, S., ed., 1968. *Karl Marx on Colonialism and Modernization.* New York: Doubleday & Company, Inc.

Goodacre, H. 2005. "William Petty and Early Colonial Roots of Development Economics." In: K. S. Jumo, ed., *The Pioneers of Development Economics: Great Economists on Development.* New Delhi/London: Tulika Books/Zed Books.

Hausmann, R., Klinger, B., and Wagner, R. 2008. "Doing Growth Diagnostics in Practice: A 'Mindbook'." Center for International Development Working Paper No. 177, Harvard University.

Hausmann, R., Rodrik, D., and Velasco, A. 2008. "Growth Diagnostics." In: N. Serra and J. E. Stiglitz, eds., *The Washington Consensus reconsidered: Towards a New Global Governance.* New York: Oxford University Press.

Hobson, J. A. 1938. *Imperialism: A Study.* London: George Allen & Unwin, Ltd.

Hodgskin, T. 1966. *Popular Political Economy.* New York: Augustus M. Kelly Publishers.

Lenin, V. 1947. "Imperialism, The Highest Stage of Capitalism." In: *The Essentials of Lenin*, Vol. 1. London: Lawrence & Wishart.

Luxemburg, R. 1951. *The Accumulation of Capital*, translated from the German by Agnes Schwarzchild. London: Routledge & Kegan Paul, Ltd.

Mill, J. S. 1904. *Principles of Political Economy with Some of their Applications to Social Philosophy.* New York: Longmans, Green, and Co.

Malthus, M. A. 1951. *Principles of Political Economy Considered with a View to Their Practical Application.* New York: Agustus M. Kelley, Inc.

Marx, K. and Engels, F. 1988. *The Communist Manifesto.* New York: Penguin.

Ricardo, D. 1933. *The Principles of Political Economy and Taxation.* London: J. M. Dent & Sons, Everyman's Library Edition.

Sen, A. K. 1982. *Poverty and Famines: An Essay on Entitlements and Deprivation.* Oxford: Clarendon Press.

Smith, A. 1908. *An Inquiry into the Nature and Causes of the Wealth of Nations.* London: George Routledge & Sons, Ltd.

Sutcliffe, B. 2008. "Marxism and Development." In: A. K. Dutt and J. Ros, eds., *International Handbook of Development Economics.* London: Edward Elgar.

Part I
Challenging the mainstream on underdevelopment and development

2 Developmentalism

Introduction

Both the theories of underdevelopment and the theories of development discussed in this chapter focus on internal causes and internal solutions.[1] Structuralism and developmentalism are often used interchangeably. Here, we view structuralism to represents a theory of underdevelopment (see Chapter 4) and developmentalism a positive agenda for development. The premise of structuralism is that underdevelopment is attributed to structural factors such as bottlenecks, rigidities and market failures. The focus of developmentalism, as practiced by developmentalist states, is to catch up with economic leaders (see Chapter 7) and developmentalist strategies are based on an understanding that certain activities employing advanced technology are more conducive to catch-up than others. Finally, developmentalists assume that once catch-up has been attained, the developmentalist state can wither even if not as completely as in Marxist state theory.[2]

While the most successful recent practitioners of developmentalism have been the East Asian economies, Reinert (p. 2) dates developmentalism back to the policies of Henry VII.[3] Developmentalists, or the pioneers of development economics discussed in this chapter, drew their inspiration from several sources and put forward multiple theories of development that are broadly referred to as developmentalist. They observed much unemployment and underemployment in underdeveloped countries and their concern with this was similar to the Keynesian preoccupation with unemployment in developed countries during the Great Depression. While the nature of the unemployment was analyzed to be different, as were the policy prescriptions, Keynes nonetheless laid the groundwork for state intervention. The idea that the state could be an agency for development was also endorsed by the Soviet Union's ability to industrialize and apparently cure its unemployment problem via a planned process over one generation. This belief in the state's ability to solve economic problems and initiate development represents the origin of the term developmentalist in the development literature; developmentalism refers to the prescriptions of developmentalist scholars.

There were important differences among the developmentalists as will be discussed below, but among the commonalities was a shared optimism. They believed that with the right policies, rapid progress was possible. Most of them believed that if the productive potential of poor countries could be tapped based on developmentalist prescriptions, economic growth and development could be attained perhaps even within a generation.

In keeping with their Keynesian inspiration, most of them adopted a macro approach to growth and development issues. Thus the concern was with aggregate variables such as saving and investment and their impact on GDP growth. Like Keynes, many developmentalists were concerned with a shortage in aggregate demand, a common theme that can be traced back to Malthus (refer to Chapter 1).

Most believed that market imperfections such as a lack of information, discontinuities due to lumpy investment and high gestation periods, inaction due to high risk, market rigidities (low supply elasticities), bottlenecks (resulting from a lack of social and physical infrastructure), and externalities were reasons for intervention.[4] Thus they advocated the need for intervention to cure these structural defects.[5] However, these economists were trained in mainstream economics and were wedded to the market approach. They prescribed a role for intervention within the market framework but not as a substitute for the market. Once it had achieved sustained growth, the government could assume the minimalist role prescribed by Adam Smith: enforcing law and order, contracts, basic regulations, and stabilization.

Most developmentalists also shared Smith's view that economic progress was more likely to occur by focusing on industry (refer to Chapter 1).[6] They viewed industry (particularly manufacturing) to be the dynamic sector of the economy and therefore the lead sector. The belief was that industrialization yielded dynamic efficiencies and other advantages unattainable in the primary sector, such as linkages with other sectors, innovation, the potential for creating technological knowledge, and the diffusion of such knowledge. These positive spillovers could be physical externalities (enter the production function as embodied technological change) or pecuniary externalities (reduced production costs for others). Other advantages included export potential as unit costs decline, learning by doing, demand-creation, employment (the first phase of industrialization was believed to be labor intensive and so would help to absorb the rural-urban migration), disembodied technological change in the form of marketing, organizational and managerial skills, modern financial and accounting practices, inculcation of modern work norms that would be diffused to the wider economy (the latter happened because machines control the pace of work and so induce work efficiency or else losses are inevitable).[7] They were welcoming of foreign investment and export growth since that could facilitate this process.

The central expectation of the developmentalists was that industrialization would absorb surplus labor, causing domestic wages to rise and improve labor's living standard while also allowing the entrepreneurial class to benefit. Essentially, this was a trickle-down view of the development process that was later challenged. This chapter reviews the thinking of scholars widely viewed to be the developmentalist pioneers.

Key thinkers

Paul Narcyz Rosenstein-Rodan (1902–1985)

Rosenstein-Rodan epitomized the big thinking of the developmentalists. His primary focus was the post-war conditions in Eastern and Southeastern Europe and the need to address their massive surplus of agrarian labor and the consequent unemployment (1943). However, his work was relevant to all backward nations at the time, since they were all confronted with a similar problem. Rosenstein-Rodan started with the presumption that industrialization was not only good for the depressed areas but also for the world as a whole via trade creation. But if development in backward areas was left to internal capital accumulation, it would entail a tremendous sacrifice of consumption in already poor areas. He noted that either capital needed to migrate to surplus labor regions or surplus labor needed to migrate to capital rich areas. However, capital flow was politically more palatable than migration and would therefore need to represent the bulk of the movement.

Rosenstein-Rodan suggested a business proposition between developed and underdeveloped countries to facilitate the movement of capital. Developed countries would finance the formation of a "trust" that would engender technology transfer and industrialization in a large area. Structural transformation and progress would result from the application of given technical knowledge rather than new technical knowledge. The business partnership between the rich and poor nations would ensure the provision of credit, machinery, and technical assistance from the rich, but also the willingness to enable the creation of some export industries in the poorer regions and perhaps the consumption of more leisure (shorter working week) in the richer nations to enable the poorer nations to pay back the loans.

Since it was preferable not to disrupt the international division of labor, the focus of industrialization would be labor intensive light manufacturing, although the complementarities would entail some heavy manufacturing also. The complementarities among the industries would also include the creating of mutual demand without which progress was not possible.[8] The creation of such mutual demand between industries would limit the disruption of world markets.

This mutuality was viewed as one of several externalities that would result, suggesting that the social marginal product of the industrialization project was greater than the private marginal product of industrial activity. This could mean, for example, that individual agents faced with labor mobility would underinvest in the provision of training and skill development. Much as Marshallian externalities from the growth of an industry accrued to individual firms, in this case the external economies from the overall industrialization project would accrue to particular industries. Specifically, the mutual assurance of aggregate demand would reduce risk and enhance expected profits. Since individual agents have limited knowledge relative to say the planning agency, the subjective risk of the firm is greater than the objective risk once the industrialization project gets underway.

Apart from facilitating training and skill development, the state would crowd in private sector activity by investing in basic industries and public utilities like railways, roads, canals, and hydro-electric power stations. The precise investment would depend on the particular constraint faced (p. 208).[9] Some of the credit would need to be used to improve agriculture in poor nations as part of the overall development strategy.

Rosenstein-Rodan's theory of development came to be widely referred to as "The Big Push," a term he employed himself, in a retrospective essay on his contribution to development economics (1984). In this retrospective, Rosenstein-Rodan conceded that some countries might in fact need a soft loan, constituting a modification of his original scheme. But he also asserted that his theory of development could, with adaptations, be relevant to underdeveloped countries in general, more than just to Eastern and Southeastern European countries.

Ragnar Nurkse (1907–1959)

Nurkse had a more elaborate theory of underdevelopment and also contributed insights on financing development and the role of trade in development, but essentially his theory of development, which he referred to as "balanced growth," was the same as Rosenstein-Rodan's "big push." Balanced growth was achieved by applying the great store of technical knowledge advantageously to industrialization in less developed countries.[10] Nurkse (1967) also assumed that deflationary excess saving was not a factor and, invoking Say's Law, suggested that a synchronized (balanced) application of capital to a whole range of industries could kick start the growth process in poor countries trapped in stagnation.

Nurkse demonstrated that stagnation resulted from low productivity on both the demand and supply sides, which was perpetuated by vicious circles (p. 4). On the supply side, low productivity resulting partly from low nutrition and ill health led to low wages, low savings, low investments, and low capital labor ratios, which kept productivity low. On the demand side, low productivity meant low wages, low aggregate demand, a small market size, low expected profits, and hence low investment, again resulting in poor productivity. The question was how to break the Gordian knot and Nurkse considered various alternatives.

He concluded that the small size of the market and poor infrastructure was not likely to attract foreign direct investment (FDI) to produce for the local market. The little FDI that came was directed towards extraction of minerals and production of primary commodities for export back to the home market. Unless the state required it, foreign companies were loath to pass on technical knowledge and managerial skills to poor countries.

He also challenged the theory of comparative advantage, with its proscription that specialization in primary commodities could provide the funds for capital accumulation. Nurkse argued this was not possible because the process would be undermined by unfavorable terms of trade, synthetic substitutes, agricultural protection in rich countries, and inelastic or stationary demand for primary goods.

Foreign grants and loans were another potential mechanism for advancing capital accumulation, but given that capital is fungible, he thought it likely that an inflow of foreign capital, either from grants or as a consequence of a positive shock in the terms of trade, would simply cause local resources to be diverted to consumption.

Ultimately, he concluded that "capital is made at home" through the implementation of appropriate policies (p. 141). But if a government had the ability to put the right policies in place, they were already beyond needing aid, and if the government had not advanced to that stage, bottlenecks would in any case reduce the absorptive capacity of aid.

There were two main barriers to obtaining an adequate amount of saving and triggering capital accumulation. For one thing, saving was deterred by low income. In addition, Nurkse found that enhanced communications encouraged low income countries to emulate the consumption patterns of high income countries so that luxury imports dissipated the scarce foreign exchange which could otherwise be used for importing capital goods and developing the industrial base.

Nurkse argued that one solution was to improve agricultural productivity, thereby releasing energy for capital construction. However, this tactic would merely create a hypothetical opportunity for capital accumulation; it would deliver development only if fiscal policies were put into place to offset the shortage of private savings by mobilizing public savings (p. 143). Such policies would be needed even in a country like Japan, which used a land tax, where the people were "indoctrinated in the virtues of thrift, businesses urged to reinvest and wages kept low" (p. 143).[11] The state could use existing or created institutions (development banks) to direct resources to private entrepreneurs and to stimulate entrepreneurial activity by providing the necessary social overhead capital including education and health. Nurkse argued that if this process was initiated, Joseph A. Schumpeter's entrepreneurs would deliver and his work "properly understood is just what the title says it is" (p. 12) i.e., a theory of economic development.

Like Rosenstein-Rodan, Nurkse recognized that many of the activities needed to get the development process underway had higher social than private returns and hence would not be forthcoming without intervention. However, he thought the debate between "planners and anti-planners" was moot because, ultimately, national characteristics such as initiative, prudence, ingenuity, and foresight were a "surer base of a nation's economic advance than the blueprints of a planning commission." Individual initiative would have to take over as the primary impetus for development.

Albert Otto Hirschman (1915–2012)

Hirschman supported development planning, but not balanced growth. He did not adhere to the notion fashionable at the time that pre-requisites such as investment in human capital, entrepreneurial and managerial capacity, technology, and public administration capacity had to be in place before the development process could commence [Rostow (1960)—discussed later in this chapter]. Hirschman suggested that development had no quantitative prerequisites, but was instead constrained by dislocations, inequalities and social tensions (1959, p. 43).

In any case, he argued that many of the proximate causes of growth were likely to be endogenous and also that the critical ingredients for progress were already present in underdeveloped countries, so that the development process was actually about calling forth "resources and abilities that are hidden, scattered, or badly utilized" (p. 5). He was less clear about what would enable this to happen and made reference to "some binding agent" (perhaps patriotism) that would get the process underway and bring it all together (p. 6).

Hirschman viewed the linkages pointed out by advocates of balanced growth as important, but thought that balanced growth was not in accordance with the actual development process, while imbalance was plausible and was also able to create opportunities that agents responded to. Like Rosenstein-Rodan and Nurkse, he pointed out that underdeveloped countries had access to a reservoir of technical progress so that inventing and innovating was not an issue. Neither was saving a constraint; excess savings or frustrated savings showed up as luxury consumption, gifts or leisure (p. 37). Investment opportunities were also plentiful, but the real issue was the ability to invest. Central to his theory of development was a theory of investment particular to underdeveloped countries.

Invariably, some sectors, industries, or activities lead the process of development and, invariably, these lead industries were found in the modern sector.[12] The modern sector bred the attitudes, skills, and abilities needed for investment. It also had the ability to mobilize the savings of the whole nation and so the classical assumption that only the capitalists saved was not warranted. The ability to invest was the absorptive capacity of the modern sector, which grew as long as this ability to invest (v) was less than the potential saving rate (s). The traditional saving-constrained model only applied after v exceeded s, and it was only then that foreign capital could help more than just in terms of the skills and abilities accompanying it (p. 36). It is also at this stage that compression of mass consumption could help. Hirschman thus characterized how the development process unfolds, suggesting that it could take many decades (p. 66).

He argued that balanced development would require the mustering of managerial and administrative skill at a level (big push) that would suggest that the country is not really underdeveloped. Therefore, development would need to rely on an alternative mechanism. In the course of development, uneven advances between sectors and industries were to be expected, and these imbalances, which consist of bottlenecks and constraints, could induce investments (pp. 62–63).[13] Addressing bottlenecks would effectively address complementarities and, thus the objective of development policy must be to give maximum play to addressing these bottlenecks (p. 43). Political survival should be enough of an inducement to address these bottlenecks and if not, this reveals that the community is not motivated by economic development.[14] Certainly, if an administration cannot address bottlenecks, they are unlikely to be able to address balanced development (p. 64).

Hirshman provided a full theory of development by specifying what activities to specialize in. He recommended those that harness complementarities or have the most linkages with other activities (particularly backward) because these activities would induce the most additional industrial activity (p. 100). The provision of social overhead capital should be driven by this objective, even though he conceded that activity could be stimulated both by excess capacity as well as shortages but that the latter is the preferred strategy since excess capacity is an invitation to invest that may not materialize.

In theory, an input-output matrix of an economy could identify activities with the greatest linkages. Imports could also be a mechanism for mapping demand, but this means that premature protection would result in a loss of important information for development planners. Once demand is identified, however, moving to local production is not straightforward. Resistance is likely to be provided by importers, foreign suppliers, consumers (at least in the short-term) and bankers who prefer to finance short term, risk free activity to industrial projects. Exports could be critical in financing imports needed for the industrialization project and in this sense the two activities complement each other (pp. 124–125).

In a retrospective essay on his development thought, Hirschman (1984, pp. 106–107) noted that the imbalance in the growth process could be antagonistic rather than benign. In other words, there could be trade-offs such that the leading sector could draw resources at the expense of the others but he thought the overall trend would be positive, though the path jagged. He conceded that along with the other development pioneers he ignored the political implications of growth theories propounded. Thus, he had not adequately anticipated Kuznets' (1955) observed imbalance between growth and equality, or that this could create antagonism and social unrest.

Arthur Lewis (1915–1991)

Lewis was characterized by Hirschman (pp. 50–51) as an advocate of balanced development and he was right in that Lewis (1954a) saw the need for a sectoral balance between industry and agriculture. However Lewis's theory of economic development does not entail any large synchronized investment and is otherwise qualitatively different from the balanced growth advocated by Rosenstein-Rodan and Nurkse. It explains the process of structural change in low income economies and also proved to be a good predictor of how that process could be impacted by policy and other changes.

Lewis's seminal article (1954a) on the dual sector economy is probably the most influential and highly cited article in development economics. While his theory may seem obvious now, it represented a major breakthrough in understanding the process of economic growth. It spawned a growth industry of articles on two sector models and dualism. In a 50-year retrospective devoted to his contribution, *The Manchester School of Economic and Social Studies* (Vol. 72, No. 6) carried his original 1954 article, along with contributions by the most prominent development economists writing half a century later. The consensus was that Lewis's was the most important paper in contributing to the emergence of development economics and that his model still had predictive relevance.

The processes Lewis modeled were rural urban migration and the associated structural change as the share of industry as a percentage of GDP expanded relative to agriculture. His model is a hybrid of classical and neo-classical theories although Lewis referred to his work as "—written in the classical tradition" (p. 400). Like classical economics, he assumed a horizontal supply of labor at a subsistence wage based on the ability to tap surplus labor in the rural sector. The demand for labor, however, was based on a downward sloping neo-classical model reflecting diminishing marginal product.[15]

Surplus labor was the central assumption and also the central concern of Lewis's model. The main source of this surplus was subsistence agriculture, but surplus labor could also emanate from the informal sectors in rural or urban economies including petty trade and services. Other sources included women entering the workforce or population growth (pp. 403–406). The puzzle was that according to conventional economic theory, the migration from rural areas should have been causing a rise in rural wages due to subsequent labor scarcity, a rise in food prices, and consequently a rise in manufacturing wages because food prices are the largest component of this wage. This would reduce manufacturing profits and reduce output and employment in the manufacturing sector hence curtailing the migration. But Lewis observed the migration was continuing without these effects and this is where surplus labor played a pivotal role in his model.

If, due to surplus labor in the agricultural sector, marginal product in agriculture is zero or close to it, the migration would result in no loss in agricultural output and no rise in food prices. In fact, Lewis argued that in some situations marginal product in agriculture could be less than zero because of overcrowding and irrational, inefficient production. In this case agricultural output would actually rise as a result of rural-urban migration. However, the central assumption of his model was not that marginal product in agriculture was zero or negative as sometimes suggested. Instead, it was the reasonable assumption that wages in agriculture were less than those prevailing in the industrial sector (p. 403).

He argued that typically, wages in industry were about 30 percent higher than the average product of labor in agriculture (the relevant concept for subsistence in income sharing households) allowing for higher productivity, cost of living, standard of living, unions, and the psychological cost of moving (p. 410). Lewis conceded that the 30 percent higher "conventional wage" (for the same quantity and quality of work) was an arbitrary number based on rough observation, but his model was applicable whenever there was a wage differential that encouraged migration.

Lewis referred to the two sectors as the capitalist and non-capitalist sectors. This is obviously not a very traditional or strictly speaking accurate terminology in the Marxian sense since Lewis included public enterprises as part of the capitalist sector.[16] In fact, his distinction was strictly between modern (capital intensive) and subsistence (labor intensive) agriculture. The producers in the modern sector could be state capitalist (state owned enterprises) or private entrepreneurs (p. 419). He was agnostic on this issue of public vs. private—as a pragmatist, he endorsed whatever worked.

Following classical economists, Lewis assumed that the source of saving is the profits of the modern sector. For Lewis, saving, capital accumulation and industrialization were the keys to development. For this reason, Lewis did not think the Keynesian framework, with its assumption of scarce labor and surplus saving, was suitable for an analysis of low income countries. In the Keynesian framework, there was an abundance of capital and other resources and the issue was putting excess capacity to use by activating the demand side (p. 401).

Anticipating Rostow (1960), Lewis posited that take-off or self-sustaining growth would occur when saving consistently reached about 12 to 15 percent of national income compared to 3 to 4 percent for a backward economy. Unlike Nurkse, low savings were not a product of low income but of a small modern sector and some countries were better than others for various reasons, including sociological, in spawning entrepreneurs who responded to opportunities (with political stability as an enabler). Once the process got underway, a virtuous circle continued to expand the modern sector as long as there was surplus labor (p. 420).

He started with a closed economy assumption but this was subsequently relaxed as will be described. Also, the two sector and two factor assumptions can be relaxed without changing model predictions. Implicit in his analysis is the assumption that the modern sector has freely available access to technology. To sum up, the horizontal supply of labor, saving by capitalists, and capital accumulation driving the growth and structural change process have classical roots. Also, since Lewis modeled a process, his model is dynamic in the classical tradition.

The process of structural change ends with the exhaustion of surplus labor as capitalists accumulate and invest. As the demand for labor then shifts to the right, the upward sloping labor supply curve of neo-classical theory becomes relevant.[17] While the model is seemingly simple, its mechanics yield many predictions pertaining to the transition from the classical to neo-classical state. For example, population growth due to an incomplete demographic transition would yield more surplus labor to draw on extending the process of capital accumulation. Education and population programs that reduce fertility more than infant mortality declines could shorten this process.

While reinvested profits of capitalists drove the process of growth and structural change, credit financing could achieve a similar outcome. Lewis argued that this would take longer and would be inflationary in the short run as consumption power is distributed to new workers. However, as credit-financed capital accumulation started to yield output, inflation would be squeezed out of the system. At this point, profits as a share of national income would rise and accumulation could become profit financed (pp. 420–422). However, in an open economy inflation could play havoc with the balance of payments and it could have other adverse consequences (p. 426).

Lewis did not distinguish between embodied and disembodied technical change since he argued that both would have the same effect (p. 413). He also recognized that many technological changes could have offsetting effects, making qualitative predictions impossible. For example, technological change could be expected to replace labor and hence extend the accumulation process, while on the other hand it could shift the demand for labor to the right and hence raise profit share. Lewis thought the latter was more likely, and assumed that surplus labor would be exhausted more quickly as the pace of capital accumulation increased.

Where Ricardo had theorized that capital accumulation was choked off by rents, Lewis explained that capital accumulation could be prematurely halted for several reasons (pp. 431–432). A social revolution would have this effect. But so, too, would a rise in conventional wage, achieved through legislation or unionization, reducing profits and reinvestment. If agricultural productivity did not keep pace with industrial productivity, the terms of trade would move in favor of agriculture. Thus as the population rose, creating greater demand for food in urban areas, rising food prices and increasing "conventional wage" would reduce profits and hence also investment. But once again, there could be offsetting effects: agricultural productivity would increase via mechanization, and the resulting decrease in food prices could be greater than the increase in agricultural wages. For the positive terms of trade effect to dominate, the income elasticity of demand for food would have to be less than one. Lewis believed that it was, based on empirical support.

Lewis believed that concern about resource scarcity and rising rents was unnecessary given the possibility of technical change in agriculture, and he argued that Ricardo and Malthus underestimated this potential. Lewis viewed the debate between Ricardo and Malthus on gluts (see Chapter 1) to be of contemporary relevance, however, and sought to resolve this debate using his model. As long as there was surplus labor at a constant wage, the surplus accruing to capitalists would rise since capitalists captured all the benefits of technical change (p. 415), yet as profits were reinvested, the wage bill and aggregate demand would rise concomitantly.

His model also yielded insights into the operations of an open economy. First, it explained that as a consequence of surplus labor, the gains of technical change in an open economy would accrue to the importing country in a competitive framework. Second, the model implied that the theory of comparative advantage required underdeveloped countries to protect manufacturing because, under conditions of surplus labor, the conventional wage was higher than the shadow wage. (pp. 443–444). Lewis also argued that in an open economy context, if quality were attained, exports could pay for cheaper food imports to offset the negative internal terms of trade effect. An open economy could also address the issue of limited internal demand for production for small economies.

Thus, the model prescriptions are to allow the terms of trade to be temporarily against agriculture to ensure cheap food and to thereby promote capital accumulation in industry. In the long run, agriculture and [industry/manufacturing] need to develop simultaneously otherwise food prices and industrial wages would rise. So an agricultural revolution must accompany an industrial revolution (p. 433). This logic also implied that prematurely raising wages via progressive institutions could hinder the growth process, a conclusion that led to criticism of the model as a trickle-down model. The initial inequality implied in the model by allowing the profit share to rise first is consistent with Kuznets' (1955) description of the growth process. Industry is the key sector in the economy and agriculture vital in a support role.

Debates about the Lewis model included one on whether Lewis's surplus labor assumption was valid. Some contested that surplus labor was inconsistent with the evidence of a secular rise in wages in urban areas. Lewis (1979) addressed this puzzle in an invited article asking him to revisit his dual economy model. Although he proposed refraining from using the term "surplus labor" since it had caused "emotional distress" (p. 211), he stood by his model and used instead the term "infinitely elastic supply of labor," though again he cautioned against making a fetish of the term since "very large" would do just as well (p. 218).

Among other explanations, he explained the rising real wages based on market segmentation into "good jobs" and "bad jobs" which, combined with the theory of non-competing groups, suggested that large firms experiencing economies of scale are willing to absorb higher rents partly as higher wages in order to buy the goodwill of the labor aristocracy. In addition, he cited various institutional explanations for the rising urban wage, including legislation and unions (pp. 223–226). In terms of his model, all of this is seen as contributing to the rising wage differential which enhances migratory pull into urban areas.[18]

Even though there is empirical support for the model, Lewis was aware that it did not work universally. For example, this might happen if the saving and investment behavior of entrepreneurs is not always consistent with modeled expectations. The model would be altered in the case of savings being dissipated through capital flight, luxury consumption, or less risky profit-making avenues like trading, real estate, speculation, and financial investments, which Lewis referred to as hoarding (p. 415).

By viewing rural-urban migration as part of the natural economic development process, the model ignored the limited carrying capacity of municipalities and hence the formation of shanty towns and the crime and exploitation that has become associated with that. Lewis (1984, p. 133) conceded in a later article that most early development economists had not foreseen the extent of the population pressure that would result from declining mortality. This trend, he observed, made the unemployment problem intractable: the creation of new employment opportunities in urban areas reinforced unemployment as it attracted more rural migrants.[19] In revisiting the dual economy model, he added that another part of the problem was that the labor absorption capacity of industrial technology was limited because it was so capital intensive (p. 222).

One way to limit the strain on urban municipalities was through land reform, which Lewis had recommended earlier, based on both equity and efficiency grounds (1984, p. 128).[20] Land Reform would generate employment in rural areas, raise agricultural productivity, create a market for industrial goods, and provide cheaper food and materials for industry. Lewis (1979, p. 217) also recommended developing agriculture with credit, extension service, irrigation, and technology.

Walt Whitman Rostow (1916–2003)

Rostow's theory of history complemented Lewis's model of structural change. Rostow became famous for his "stages of growth" description of the historical progression from poor to rich country status. Rostow (1960) proposed a linear historical progression but not one based on any underlying conceptual framework. This was posed as an alternative to the Marxian theory of historical materialism, which was based on Hegelian dialectics and conceptualized the progression from one stage to another as the result of social contradictions which, through their creation and resolution, propelled the onward march of history through various stages including feudalism, capitalism, socialism, and communism. While the stages were linear, Marx himself did not consider that historical movement had to be linear.

Rostow proffered a theory of history as a descriptive framework based on a study of European history. He lumped the early stages together as traditional society, and identified the other stages respectively as pre-conditions for take-off, drive to maturity, and mass consumption. While developed countries were in the most advanced stage, the second and third stages describe the growth process in underdeveloped countries and are therefore particularly relevant for this book.

According to Rostow, one of the pre-conditions for take-off was the need for modern science to shape the production function in both agriculture and industry for cost reductions (p. 20). Because traditional society was characterized as pre-scientific and subject to feudal control, changes in production structures would need to be accompanied by changes in attitudes towards fundamental and applied science, and by new methods of training individuals to operate in disciplined social and industrial organizations.

Other pre-conditions included the development of financial, political and social institutions resulting from the displacement of feudal society, perhaps due to colonialism as suggested by Marx (see Chapter 1). Colonialism "could not avoid" bringing about a transformation in thought, knowledge, and institutions. In addition, colonialism supplied social overhead capital such as ports, docks, roads, and railways, which moved society along a transitional path (p. 27).[21] In addition, colonialism could provoke "reactive nationalism to colonial humiliation" bringing about the right leadership for society to progress (p. 26).

Furthermore, financial development that would provide credit to industry and agriculture needed to play a central role. The institutional development should be accompanied by appropriate social and physical infrastructure and management skills. Resources for these social investments would come from rising productivity in extractive and primary commodity production (p. 21). Like Lewis, he viewed agriculture as key to providing food, materials, revenue, markets, and foreign exchange for industrial sector development (pp. 22–23).

Rostow believed that take-off would finally occur once a modern manufacturing base was established and investment exceeded about 10 percent of GDP, signaling that output growth had surpassed population growth (p. 20, p. 39). This process would result from a virtuous cycle in which social overhead capital would contribute to agricultural and manufacturing growth, exports would increase foreign exchange earnings, and profits/tax revenues would be ploughed back into investments for further growth as in the Lewis model. His retrospective (Rostow, 1984) recognized the long term cyclical (Kondratieff) swings in energy, food and commodity prices and the need for North-South cooperation in addressing these scarcities as well as evident environmental problems.

Assessment of developmentalist thought

A careful reading of the pioneers indicates that they were quite aware of what their critics charged them with for having missed out on. Their focus on capital accumulation, following from classical scholars, led critics to accuse them of having neglected other important factors. For example, they were aware of the need for institutional pre-requisites although Hirschman argued that these were likely to be endogenous to the development process. One important commonality was the view that industrialization is central to the growth process because dynamic efficiencies are more likely to be inherent in this sector than others. Notwithstanding this conviction, they were aware of the complementary role that the agricultural sector needed to play. Lewis argued that growth would be constrained unless the industrial revolution was accompanied by an agricultural revolution, and Rosenstein-Rodan and Nurkse also emphasized the importance of agriculture. While they supported the case for import substitution industrialization (ISI) on the basis of trade theory, these market economists allowed competition and efficiency to take center stage in their work. Nor did their support of ISI preclude exports or openness; for example, Hirschman viewed exporting and ISI as complementary activities and Lewis also viewed the latter to follow logically from the former.

One apparent oversight in developmentalist thinking was not anticipating that industrialization would be unable to absorb the labor surplus in many LICs, although there were exceptions as indicated above. Lewis attributed this to the partial demographic transition and pointed out in retrospect that population growth combined with a rate of rural-urban migration that exceeded the rate of urban job creation exacerbated unemployment. He conceded that, as a result, the race to provide livelihoods for a population may be lost in many cases.

One could charge the developmentalist pioneers for having a trickle-down approach. Capital intensive industrialization, market concentration, low wages due to surplus labor, and unemployment generated inequalities. Economic power led to political power and business elites also got enriched by low taxes and tax evasion, and subsidies. Thus the income share of the bottom 40 percent fell and in many cases the drive up the inverted U-shaped Kuznets curve was not forthcoming (Aluwalia, 1974). Again, there was an awareness of this as a potential problem; the political instability that such inequalities could generate was viewed as possibly blocking the growth and structural transformation process.

Developmentalists also commonly prescribed a significant role for the state and policy planning due to various market failures. However, once again, Lewis argued "In countries where government is corrupt and inefficient, laissez faire, laissez passer is the best recipe for economic growth" (1954b, p. 83). Similarly Nurske pointed out that the initiative, prudence and ingenuity of a people trumps the blueprints of planning commissions.

Summary and conclusions

The ideas of the developmentalists were influential and, while their theories were discredited during the heyday of the free-market economics in the 1980s, there has been a reassessment (Chapter 7). Indeed, many economists have pointed out that the interventionist period prior to 1980 delivered a higher growth rate in Latin America, Africa and Asia or built a base on which later growth was built. Scholars have pointed out that developmentalist theory can be applied to explain the East Asian economic growth miracles. However, this may still be a minority view with the mainstream economists preferring non-interventionist free market principles as explanations. Even so, the developmentalists have established a prominent place for themselves in the history of macro development economics thought as the pioneers and big thinkers.

Rosenstein-Rodan diagnosed the two problems confronting underdeveloped nations to be capital shortage and the lack of purchasing power, and the concept of a "big-push" program based on planned and complementary industrialization gained much traction. He noted that one factory could not succeed due to the lack of purchasing power and complementary inputs. But if the state used foreign loans to set up a range of complementary industries, these industries would confer externalities on the production and consumption sides, since employment and income would create the needed mutual demand.

The big push was implicit in the Marshall Plan that was effective in reconstructing war torn Western Europe.[22] Rosenstein-Rodan premised a role for the state based on the need to correct externalities or market failures in cases where the social marginal product of an activity exceeded the private marginal product. Socially sub-optimal outcomes resulted for several reasons. First, private entrepreneurs faced higher risk and lower expected profits than they would have, given a balanced industrial program that reinforced both the supply and demand sides. Second, individual agents were limited by the information they possessed relative to a larger planning agency. Third, social overhead capital with long gestation periods could crowd in private sector activities. Fourth, given labor mobility, the private sector would underinvest in training and skill development. With appropriate intervention, however, these socially sub-optimal outcomes could be reversed.

Although Nurkse's theory of development and associated prescriptions were virtually the same as Rosenstein-Rodan's, his theory of underdevelopment was original. Nurkse argued that developing countries were trapped in vicious circles on both the demand and supply sides. On the demand side, low income meant low aggregate demand and so low capital accumulation, low productivity, and low income. On the supply side, low income and low nutrition meant low productivity, low wages, low savings, and hence low investment and productivity. Seeing that both of these cycles discouraged savings, which he viewed as the critical ingredient for capital accumulation and economic growth, Nurkse examined various options that might enable an LIC to break out of these vicious circles.

In addition to low incomes, emulating the consumption standards of developed countries also resulted in a leakage of foreign exchange needed for capital goods imports. Nurkse doubted that specializing in primary commodities in accordance with the theory of comparative advantage would yield the necessary capital. He posited that the terms of trade would remain unfavorable under such a policy due to the low income elasticity of demand for primary commodities and the availability of synthetic substitutes. Foreign direct investment was also unlikely to be the source of needed capital since an impoverished market was unlikely to attract capital for domestic production. Aid, grants or loans, on the other hand, might simply allow local funds to be diverted into consumption. Ultimately, the process needed to be indigenous and endogenous, and an opportunity could be created if underdeveloped countries could "mine the energy released" from developing the productive potential of agriculture. This required appropriate fiscal effort. But the state needed only to get the process going with credit and sufficient social overhead capital to crowd in the private sector and then step out of the way. Only the Schumpeterian entrepreneurial process could sustain economic growth once kick-started and this is how he interpreted the economic growth process of Japan.

Hirschman argued that if underdeveloped countries had the organizational and managerial capacity to handle the "big push" of balanced growth, they would not really be underdeveloped. In practice, the process of development is not characterized by balance, but by imbalance, and these imbalances create opportunities in sustaining the process of development. When certain activities progress faster than others in industry, shortages of key inputs and materials are created and the subsequent rise in prices stimulate further market activity. Industries that moved ahead would reduce prices and encourage downstream activity. Further, bottlenecks would create pressure and induce policy makers to respond and the social overhead capital provided would crowd in further activity.

Hirschman argued that industries have both upstream and downstream linkages called "forward" (towards final product) and "backward" (towards primary commodities). Thus, it would make sense to pick industries with the highest linkages such as steel (would encourage coal and iron upstream and engineering goods, automobiles, bikes, and a range of industries downstream). He argued that these industries are inherently capital intensive, but once the linkages are accounted for their overall contribution to employment would be no less than small scale, labor intensive alternatives.

Like other developmentalists, Hirschman was very optimistic about the possibilities of growth and development in the poor countries. He argued that the real issue was not finding the optimum use of existing resources, but rather being able to harness the hidden, badly utilized, and scattered productive potential of underdeveloped countries. The wherewithal for development, including savings, was present and the challenge was the ability to invest. While Hirschman associated Lewis with the advocates of balanced development, one could argue that his writings were complementary to the Lewis model. While Lewis dealt with industrial sector investment with a broad brush as part of the process of structural change that enhanced the share of industry in GDP, Hirschman provided many details regarding the mechanics of investment within the sector.

Lewis is probably the pioneer who has had the greatest impact on the field of development economics. He modeled the process of economic growth and structural change in low income countries and his parsimonious and simple model lent itself to rich analysis, extension and predictive power. Although the analysis had many critics, many were off base. His model in a nutshell stated that, assuming surplus labor, capitalists can claim a surplus that they can reinvest to generate economic growth. This process will continue until the labor surplus is exhausted, at which point the economy can no longer be appropriately modeled using a quasi-classical model, but instead lends itself to neo-classical analysis. Lewis identified many possible blockages to the growth process and his model is also able to predict what would happen to the growth process due to changes in technology, population, education and trade.

Chenery *et al.* (1986) explored the nature of the structural change that would be predicted by Lewis's model and their stylized facts validated Lewis's predictions. Country case studies also provide support for the Lewis model, showing that, as surplus labor was exhausted in the newly industrialized economies of East Asia, wages rose, and these countries lost market share to the next tier of industrializing economies (Malaysia, Thailand, and Indonesia). These countries were subsequently displaced by China. Press reports now (2012) suggest that rising wages in China are enabling economies like Vietnam, Cambodia, and Bangladesh to contest market share in the labor intensive textile and leather industries. Thus, as some Asian countries confront rising labor costs and move up the value chain, they create a "flying geese" pattern where other Asian neighbors assumed the leadership lower down in the value chain.[23] Lewis's theory stood the test of time and he was awarded a Nobel Prize for his insightful work in 1969.

Rostow classified and fleshed out the process of structural change that Lewis modeled and perhaps his most abiding contributions are his historical and multi-disciplinary approach and the terminology he coined. Rostow gained much stature but also drew harsh criticism. His main contribution was a synthesis, since much of what he proffered had already been written by earlier developmentalists. It was also not clear how and why the pre-conditions would emerge, for although Rostow hypothesized that colonialism would play a central role, other scholars have argued that colonialism actually reinforced feudalism and arrested the growth process rather than contributed to it (see Chapters 3 and 4). Given the high population growth rate, the threshold of investment reaching 10 percent of GDP was not likely to be enough to absorb the labor force as subsequently became evident. Rostow's attempt to analyze similarities between the development path of developed and underdeveloped countries was also refuted since the initial conditions for developed countries were very different from those faced by underdeveloped countries [see Myrdal (1956, p. 170)].

Despite these criticisms, Rostow has been influential. He successfully identified the important pre-conditions that needed to accompany capital accumulation. Although not the only social thinker to place technology center stage, he joined a celebrated group. In addition, his narrative is rich by drawing on the interaction of the economic with the institutional, social, political and historical. This narrative breathes life into complex processes the outcomes of which are parameters like capital and technology that he argued become the sole objects of sterile manipulation by economists. His lasting influence is evidenced by the fact that the terminology he developed for his model is still used.

Going back and reading the pioneers in development economics is humbling since these scholars seem to have said it all six or seven decades ago. Much of the critique of these pioneers appears to be a caricature. A careful reading of their work reveals they were market friendly, aware of the need for a productive agriculture, and adopted a nuanced view of import substitution industrialization. They were also well aware that what they proposed was no magic bullet. For example, Nurkse put forward the importance of domestic resource mobilization and capital accumulation based on mining agricultural productivity while recognizing that country specificities such as human endowments, social attitudes, historical accidents, and political conditions are all critical. Thus he was clear that there can be "no standard recipe of universal applicability" (p. 150). At the same time, it is clear that if everything counts, one is left without a theory. The developmentalists, for their part, managed to put forward theories of underdevelopment and development that still have resonance.

Notes

1 Development here refers to generalized wellbeing. Structuralists and developmentalists used development and economic growth interchangeably whereas a distinction was made later as explained in Chapter 5.
2 Mainstream classical scholars, developmentalists and neo-classical economists do not flesh out a theory of the state while it is central to the analysis of structuralists, dependency theorists, Marxists, and radical political economists. A working definition could be that the state is the seat of power that enables legislation and administration but questions of whose interest is served, legitimacy and political change are not addressed by this definition.
3 For a brief review of developmentalism and the developmentalist state refer to Khan (2010, pp. 44–45).

4 Young's (1928) focus on disequilibrium, external economies, increasing returns, and industry as an aggregate was a precursor to some of this thinking.

5 Ghosh (p. 116) attributes the identification of these key structural differences between developed and developing countries to Michal Kalecki.

6 This includes manufacturing (generally the largest component), and also utilities, communications, transportation, and mining.

7 These ideas are of course consistent with the increasing returns modeled by endogenous growth theorists [Lucas (1988); Romer (1994)] rather than the constant returns of the Solow (1956) growth model. The World Bank (2005, p. 43) explains why the contribution of new growth theory to development economics has been modest. Krugman (1998) notes that the ideas of the developmentalists would have received more attention and had more staying power if their method had been more formal. For an example of a later formalization refer to Murphy, Schleifer, and Vishny (1989).

8 The classical influence is evident both in the centrality of capital accumulation and aggregate demand. While Malthus brought the latter concept center stage in his analysis, Keynes' exploration of this concept in the 1930s took the profession by storm.

9 This insight is the basis of "growth diagnostics" put forward by Hausmann, Rodrik, and Valesco (2008).

10 He preferred the terms low, middle and high income, much later adopted by the World Bank, but adopted accepted usage.

11 Thus he argued that, contrary to Keynesian theory pertaining to recessions in developed countries, thrift may serve underdeveloped countries well.

12 There is no theory posited regarding the emergence and size of the modern sector.

13 Hirschman clarified that given the very different context, this concept of induced investment is very different from the Keynesian concept of investment being induced by an increase in national income.

14 It may be that the leadership, even if civilian, has its own short term plutocratic agenda and therefore not responsive to community pressure expressed via the ballot.

15 His model very closely resembles the Ricardian model except that the latter had land as the third factor since Ricardo was concerned by rising rents choking off capital accumulation. While the downward sloping marginal productivity of land was based on the declining returns to the less fertile pieces of land in Ricardo's model, for Lewis the demand for labor sloped down due to the neo-classical factor proportions model suggesting declining marginal productivity of labor holding capital constant.

16 Some asides in his paper suggest that Lewis did not have a strong understanding of Marx's theories of exploitation or crisis (p. 405, p. 435).

17 Fei and Ranis (1964) formalized, elaborated, and extended Lewis's dual sector economy model.

18 Casual empiricism would certainly suggest to those living in many LICs that surplus labor in the urban informal sector is often fed by rural areas. Rigorous estimates using different methods have varied with one study for India suggesting that over 20 percent of Indian agricultural labor is surplus on farm sizes of 20 acres or less (Rosenzweig and Foster, 2010).

19 Harris and Todaro (1968) formalized this insight and explained the puzzle of rural-urban migration persisting despite urban unemployment in terms of subjective probability of getting an urban sector job exceeding the objective probability of doing so. In so doing, they shifted the focus of attention from industrialization to rural development since more rural jobs would obviate the need to move.

20 Whether or not small farmers are more efficient (the efficiency argument for land redistribution) remains contested in the literature.

21 This view of colonialism contrasts with that put forward by radical scholars as indicated in Chapters 1, 3, and 4 of this book and unlike them Rostow makes no distinction between colonialism and imperialism.

22 Of course, as many have pointed out, a major cause of the success of the Marshall Plan was that the social and institutional pre-conditions for rebuilding were already in place in Europe.
23 This pattern of international production restructuring was developed as a descriptive model and referred to as the "flying geese" paradigm by Akamatsu (1962).

References

Akamatsu, K. 1962. "A historical pattern of economic growth in developing countries." *Journal of Developing Economies*, 1 (1), 3–25.

Aluwalia, M. S. 1974. "Income inequality: Some dimensions of the problem." In: H. B. Chenery *et al.* eds. *Redistribution with Growth*. London: Oxford University Press.

Chenery, H., Robinson, S., and Syrquin, M. 1986. *Industrialization and Growth: A Comparative Study*. New York: Oxford University Press.

Fei, J. C. H. and G. Ranis, 1964. *Development of the Labor Surplus Economy*. Homewood, Illinois: Richard Irwin.

Ghosh, J. 2005. "Michael Kalecki and the Economics of Development." In: K. S. Jumo, ed., *The Pioneers of Development Economics: Great Economists on Development*. New Delhi/London: Tulika Books/Zed Books.

Harris, J. R. and Todaro, M. P. 1968. "A Two Sector Model of Migration with Urban Unemployment in Developing Countries." Massachusetts Institute of Technology, Department of Economics, Working Paper 33.

Hausmann, R., Rodrik, D., and Velasco, A. 2008. "Growth Diagnostics." In: N. Serra and J. E. Stiglitz, eds., *The Washington Consensus Reconsidered: Towards a New Global Governance*. New York: Oxford University Press.

Hirschman, A. O. 1984. "The Formative Period." In: G. M. Meier and D. Steers, eds., *Pioneers in Development*. New York: Oxford University Press.

Hirschman, A. O. 1959. *The Strategy of Economic Development*. New Haven: Yale University Press.

Khan, S. R. 2010. "Exploring and naming an economic development alternative." Chapter 1. In: Khan, S. R. and J. Christiansen, eds., *Market as Means Rather than Master: Towards New Developmentalism*. New York: Routledge.

Kuznets, S. 1955. "Economic Growth and Income Inequality." *American Economic Review,* 45 (1), 1–28.

Krugman, P. 1998. "The Fall and Rise of Development Economics: *Development Geography and Economic Theory*. Cambridge, Mass: MIT Press.

Lewis, W. A. 1984, "Development Economics in the 1950s." In: G. M. Meier and D. Seers, eds., *Pioneers in Development.* New York: Oxford University Press.

Lewis, W. A. 1979. "The Dual Economy Revisited." *The Manchester School of Economic and Social Studies*, 47 (3), 211–229.

Lewis, W. A. 1954a. "Economic Development with Unlimited Supplies of Labor." *The Manchester School of Economic and Social Studies,* 22, May, 139–153. Reprinted in: A. N. Agarwal and S. P. Singh, eds., 1958. The *Economics of Underdevelopment*. New York: Oxford University Press, 400–449.

Lewis, W. A. 1954b. *The Theory of Economic Growth*. Homewood Illinois: Irwin.

Lucas, R. E. 1988. "On the Mechanism of Economic Development." *Journal of Monetary Economics*, 22 (1), 3–42.

Meier, G. M. and Seers, D. 1984. *Pioneers in Development*. New York: Oxford University Press.

Murphy, K. M., Schleifer, A., and Vishny, R. W. 1989. "Industrialization and the Big Push." *Journal of Political Economy*, 97 (5), 1003–1025.

Myrdal, G. 1956. *An International Economy*. New York: Harper & Brothers Publishers.

Nurkse, R. 1967. *Problems of Capital Formation in Underdeveloped Countries and Patterns of Trade and Development*. New York: Oxford University Press.

Reinert, E. S. 2010. "Developmentalism." Working Papers in Technology, Governance and Economic Dynamics No. 34. The Other Canon Foundation, Norway.

Romer, P. M. 1994. "The Origins of Endogenous Growth." *Journal of Economic Perspectives*, 8 (1), 3–22.

Rosenstein-Rodan, P. N. 1984. "Natura Facit Saltum: Analysis of Disequilibrium Growth Process." In: G. M. Meier and D. Seers, eds., *Pioneers in Development*. New York: Oxford University Press.

Rosenstein-Rodan, P. N. 1943. "The Problems of Industrialization of Eastern and South-Eastern Europe." *The Economic Journal*, 53 (210/211), 202–211.

Rosenzweig, M. and Foster, A. D. 2010. "Is There Surplus Labor in Rural India?" Yale University Economic Growth Center Discussion Paper No. 991, New Haven, www.econ.yale.edu/~egcenter/

Rostow, W. W. 1960. *The Stages of Economic Growth: A Non-Communist Manifesto*. Cambridge: Cambridge University Press.

Rostow, W. A. 1984. "Development: The Political Economy of the Marshallian Long Period" In G. M. Meier and D. Seers, eds., *Pioneers in Development*. New York: Oxford University Press.

Solow, R. 1956. "A Contribution to the Theory of Economic Growth." *Quarterly Journal of Economics*, 70 (1), 65–94.

World Bank. 2005. *Economic Growth in the 1990s: Learning from a Decade of Reform*. Washington, D.C.: World Bank.

Young, A. A. 1928. "Increasing Returns and Economic Progress." *The Economic Journal*, 38 (152), 527–542.

3   Neo-Marxism and the political economy of development

Introduction

As indicated in Chapter 1 (en. 12), Marx viewed capitalism as a powerful force for developing society's productive potential. However, the capital accumulation that generated this development he viewed as based on the exploitation of workers by the capitalists. Marx predicted that this social injustice would destroy capitalism. Class was central in Marx's analysis and, unsurprisingly, the neo-Marxian branch of development economics revolves around the issues of class and social injustice in alternative contexts.

Paul Baran's work served as a bridge from Marx to radical thinking in general and to neo-Marxist development economics in particular. There is an echo of his seminal writing in much of Latin structuralism and radical political economy of development. Similar to structuralism (Chapter 4), Baran's analysis and neo-Marxist thought focus on the internal and external causes of both underdevelopment and development. The emphasis on internal or external causes varies by scholars.

Thinkers

Paul Baran (1909–1964)

In *The Political Economy of Growth* (1957) Baran put forward the concept of neo-colonialism, drawing on earlier theories of colonialism and imperialism as well as his observations on the state of the world in the 1940s and 1950s. Neo-colonialism posed a major challenge to economic development in newly independent countries, since the advanced countries' need for raw materials and investment outlets meant that they would bitterly oppose the industrialization that was essential for development in the newly independent countries (p. 14). Baran argued that underdevelopment resulted not simply from the lack of capital but also from outdated political, social, and economic institutions (p. 2) and these could not be taken as a given, as done in neo-classical economics, since economic development would involve changing these (p. 4). Such transformation was opposed and resisted by the West, which allied itself with local retrograde forces which benefited from the status quo and also facilitated the presence and profit repatriation of Western multinationals (p. 14).

Baran defined actual economic surplus as the gap between society's output and its essential consumption. Potential economic surplus is the gap between output and essential consumption in a rationally structured society (pp. 22–23). Essential consumption was defined in terms of meeting what later came to be called basic human needs (p. 30) (see Chapter 5).[1]

Colonialism was identified as the cause of backwardness in underdeveloped countries. The forcible shift of colonial production to a focus on export crops destroyed the self-sufficiency of agrarian pre-capitalist societies, while the withering competition from exported manufactured goods destroyed rural handicrafts (p. 142). Infrastructure was established to serve colonial exporting interests (p. 143). Capital accumulation by locals was retarded and surplus was transferred to the colonial countries by manipulating terms of trade, direct transfers, and taxes (p. 146). As pointed out by Rosa Luxemburg (Chapter 1), pre-colonial society was destroyed by colonialism.

Explaining British colonialism in India, Baran summarized that land and taxation policy ruined the village economy, while commercial policy ruined the artisan and generated massive labor surplus. Finally, economic policy ruined incipient industrial development. The local beneficiaries of colonialism included rent-seekers like landlords, money lenders, petty merchants and businesses, middlemen, and speculators. In his words, "Sharks of all description proliferated whose interests were tied to the British" (p. 149).

Post-colonial societies inherited a system of low-productivity peasant agriculture in which landlords appropriated the surplus and engaged in the kind of luxury consumption that classical economists railed against (p. 164). Agricultural improvements yielded slow returns and, in any case, imperfect capital markets made loans for such investments prohibitive (p. 166). Thus money lending was found to be more rewarding than productive investments and the purpose of land acquisition was status (p. 167). Surplus was also appropriated by other rentiers, merchants, and intermediaries who did not provide a dynamic impetus to the economy (p. 170).

Baran also documented the evolution of capitalism from a competitive phase during the era of the classical economists to monopoly capitalism at the turn of the twentieth century (p. 59). A vast amount of investable surplus was generated in this monopoly capitalistic phase and with government backing unutilized surplus was invested abroad to secure materials and markets in the underdeveloped countries while they were in their weakened, post-colonial condition (p. 113). Tied loans and grants and technical assistance, backed by potential military force, became an important mechanism for securing advantage (p. 122).

Foreign capital investment in materials was highly mechanized and most of the inputs and equipment for extraction were imported. Relative to the profits generated and repatriated, this capital infusion was modest. The "enclave" nature of the operations meant that even many of the consumer goods for local workers were imported (pp. 178–183). The investments in plantations perpetuated food insecurity relative to what would be forthcoming from a diversified agriculture (p. 187).

Baran challenged each element of the case for foreign direct investment (FDI): namely, that the surplus transferred is created by FDI, some is locally retained, and infrastructure development facilitated (p. 185). He argued that FDI only exploited the resource that generated the surplus. Also, the mechanics of surplus creation, such as in the case of sugar plantation agriculture in northeast Brazil, was based on exploitation, pauperization, and annihilation of large parts of indigenous production (p. 186). Rich and fertile land that was abundant in forests and fruit trees was stripped. The subsequent shortages of fruits, greens, and vegetables created food insecurity. Much of Latin America, Africa, and Asia suffered from such "one track" exploitation, which resulted in depletion and impoverishment (p. 188). Baran argued that in due course local resource extraction would have been possible and all the surplus created locally retained (p. 186).

As was true of the colonial infrastructure, much of the FDI-induced infrastructure only served the purpose of exploiting natural resources (p. 192). In any case, Baran argued that articulated infrastructure does not lead to industrial capitalism, but vice versa (p. 193). Local beneficiaries of the FDI were mostly a handful of "comprodores" (local business associates). He argued that the principal effect of multinational corporations (MNCs) in underdeveloped countries was to strengthen the sway of feudalists, merchants and monopoly capitalists to the exclusion of indigenous industrial capitalists (pp. 194–195). Competition from the latter would raise wages and other input costs and hence negatively impact MNC profits (p. 197).

In support of this argument, Baran documented the pronouncements of senior US policy makers, including Presidents, who had emphasized the importance of ensuring a hospitable business climate for MNCs (p. 199). Private foreign capital would be "aided and abetted" by a country's home government, which would use "all possible means" to obtain concessions that could subsequently be generalized to other US based MNCs. Baran also cited specific comments showing that social services in the post-colonial countries were designed to improve the quality of labor for foreign capital; meanwhile, expenditures on these services were externalized to aid programs and local administrations (p. 200). Vast sums were spent on the maintenance of sprawling bureaucracies and military establishments with Western aid money going to prop up friendly regimes and preserve the social order and MNC privileges (p. 215).

In "On the Political Economy of Backwardness" (1973) Baran elaborated on why underdevelopment persisted in underdeveloped countries. He noted that in underdeveloped countries, the middle class attempted to secure privileges by aligning with feudal, monopolistic businesses and obscurantist forces, rather than opposing these groups, as had the middle classes in developed societies (p. 93). The threat of socialism in the Cold War era reinforced this accommodation (p. 94). This alliance preserved social stability but also backwardness. The backwardness was reinforced by the class behavior of the ruling elites.

Conspicuous consumption, including foreign travel, by the feudal class matched by that of the monopolistic business class left little surplus for capital accumulation. The incentive for the latter was in any case blunted by the massive wealth and income inequality that curbed effective demand (p. 96) and by the latent political instability implied by the high degree of social injustice (p. 98). Because monopolistic businesses with a colonial merchant mentality sought quick returns, these businesses avoided building the industrial base that would improve agriculture by providing the needed utilities, machinery and materials, and would also absorb the surplus labor released as agriculture modernized (pp. 96–97). Primary exports were an avenue for investment but this was left to MNCs which possessed the capital for large scale operations, the ability and willingness to assume the risk entailed in long term projects and the requisite marketing knowledge (p. 96).

A possible alternative route to industrialization that Baran considered was the state using progressive taxation and channeling the surplus to productive physical and human investments to crowd in the private sector (p. 98), as recommended by the developmentalists (Chapter 2). Baran doubted that this could happen. The lack of a competent, honest civil service in underdeveloped countries contributed negligibly to his doubts. The main issue was that the fundamental reforms needed would be opposed by the political and social structure of the government in power. Progressive agrarian reforms, progressive taxation, curbs on capital flight and luxury consumption, and curbing monopolistic practices by extending the industrial base would be opposed by the vested interests of the governing elites (p. 100). Baran's pessimistic summation was that the "keepers of the past cannot be the builders of the future (p. 102)." His dire warning was that if the capitalist middle classes did not opt to reward the "efficient, able, and industrious" by supporting progressive, competitive capitalism, they would instead face a social revolution leading to authoritarian planning and social collectivism (p. 102).

Celso Furtado (1920–2004)

Furtado (1964) extended class analysis to the Latin American context, specifically to Brazil. He argued that accumulation in advanced capitalist societies is achieved when the business elites appropriate a substantial part of the increased product. In addition, the impulse for increased living standards by the masses is harnessed and their consumption patterns gradually diversified by business elites (p. 48). The destruction of the handicraft economy provides the unlimited supply of labor but, as accumulation proceeds, labor bargaining power and hence labor share of product is enhanced. This process can be deferred, however, by technological change that serves the interests of capital (p. 49).

In post-colonial societies, the technology is borrowed to create a modern sector, which initially results in a dual economy. As craft production is eliminated the capitalists benefit from the unlimited supply of cheap labor. In Brazil, industrialization benefited from this surplus labor but industry really emerged as a by-product of the defense of the exporting interests of the large feudal estates. The exchange rate needed to be overvalued to protect coffee prices (p. xvii).

This provided industrialists with the opportunity to expand capacity. Furtado was also aware that the process of industrialization was distorted and he noted that perverse incentives for capital use in a surplus labor economy led to a speculative excess capacity. Also, the "non-essential" goods confronting import barriers provided a perverse incentive for local production.[2]

Furtado's definition of economic development as "incorporating and diffusing new techniques" (p. 47) was similar to Singer's (Chapter 4). But, much of Furtado's analysis of the dynamic of development in post-colonial societies was framed as the struggle for class dominance. The contending classes were land owners, traders and financiers allied to foreign interests, and capitalists producing for the domestic market (p. 67). The state was the arena where competing interests were contested.[3] The landed class was pro-trade but anti-state in that the status quo was one in which they were dominant and the state was a channel through which other interests were also mediated. All classes needed the state to facilitate their activities and to provide urban services (p. 68). The state consequently expanded and developed a salaried middle class. Beneath these classes were the workers and peasants. In the struggle for political control, the masses were often used by populist demagogues to discipline rival elite factions.[4] Furtado was concerned that one possible path society and the economy can adopt is that of rent-seeking as the main impulse of entrenched power. If so, society would stagnate and social movements would become the only mechanism for social development.[5]

In "The Brazilian Model of Development" (1973) Furtado deconstructed effective demand and the nature of industrialization emerging from that. A key point was his distinction between modernization (a more diversified consumption basket) and development (effective technological learning based productive processes) (pp. 325–326). In Brazil's case, primary exports enabled modernization by raising the average income of the feudal elites. Given Brazil's size and potential for scale economies, MNCs had the technology and incentive to cater to this elite's effective demand since this consumption pattern merely emulated that of the rich world. In this regard, the technological cost of extending production to a different locale by MNCs was marginal; wages were low due to surplus labor and profit rates high.

Unlike MNCs, local industry could not cater to the diversified consumption basket of the rich because it lacked the technology access. Therefore local industry catered to the restricted consumption basket of mainly non-durable goods of the rest of the population. While the market size for these goods was stagnant due to low wages, Brazil was large enough that scale economies and externalities could be achieved through state-subsidized exports. Thus the concentration of income in Brazil yielded a lopsided production structure but also high growth rates (pp. 327–328).

Arghiri Emmanuel (1911–2001)

Emmanuel (1972) extended Marxian analysis to explore international trade. He contended that this task was one that Marx had planned but was unable to get to.[6] Emmanuel launched a comprehensive challenge to Ricardo's theory of comparative advantage by arguing that prices were determined by factor costs rather than by productivity, and that specialization was not premised on natural advantage.[7] Most importantly, he showed that international trade between developed and underdeveloped countries represented unequal exchange or exploitation via a transfer of surplus from the latter to the former. He did not view this surplus transfer to be dependent on what is produced by underdeveloped countries i.e. primary rather than manufactured commodities (p. xxx). He argued that, as far as examining the dynamics of trade, the most realistic premise was that capital is mobile and labor is not. This premise differs from the factor immobility premise of mainstream trade models, including Ricardo's theory of comparative advantage. Emmanuel reasoned that if capital is mobile, profit rates are equalized but wages are not (p. xxxiii). This reversed Ricardo's premise of international trade being based on equal wages but unequal profit rates (p. 266).

In the first chapter of his work, Emmanuel established the mechanisms via which prices are dependent on wages. In his second chapter he established that capital is sufficiently mobile for profit rates to be equalized, but also demonstrated divergence between wages in developed and underdeveloped countries (pp. 46–47).[8] He argued that wages represented the independent variable and were not determined like other market prices. His third chapter demonstrated that wages were higher in developed countries due to biological (nutrition needs), historical (traditions, habits, custom, morals), social (legislation), and institutional (trade unions) reasons (pp. 126–128).[9] In underdeveloped countries, labor surplus kept wages at the subsistence level (p. 89).[10]

Wage inequality led to exploitation or a net transfer of surplus value from underdeveloped to developing countries. Emmanuel showed that, at prices that equalize profits, underdeveloped countries exported products that embody a larger number of labor hours in return for imported products that embody far fewer hours of equivalent skill (pp. 61–62).[11] This resulted in a vicious cycle since poor countries were deprived of the ability to accumulate and continued to stagnate. Wages stayed low while the narrow market created a disincentive to invest leaving a pool of surplus labor (p. 131).

Emmanuel went on to discuss a number of ways of breaking out of this vicious cycle, such as by pursuing regional integration. Trade between countries with similar wage structures would reduce exploitative unequal exchange (p. 147). Export taxes in underdeveloped countries would also reduce unequal exchange by limiting trade (p. 233). Regional trade agreements among underdeveloped countries that enabled industrialization and diversification would also help; by reducing dependence on imports from developed countries, underdeveloped countries could reduce unequal exchange and improve their terms of trade.[12] He realized that the adverse terms of trade and adjustment costs thus imposed on developed countries would produce ferocious resistance. Indeed, he argued that trade rules are set, monitored and enforced by international financial institutions like the IMF and World Bank, and GATT (later the WTO) in order to prevent this situation, and to protect developed country interests. (p. 268).

Emmanuel defined underdevelopment as the gap between what the means of production could potentially deliver, given the current state of technology, compared to what was actually produced (p. 207).[13] He argued that wage increases can precede development. For example, colonies in temperate zones like the USA, Canada, Australia, and New Zealand inherited Britain's high wage structure, which proved to be an advantage in creating an internal market, and development followed later.[14] He concluded that the solution for the initial lack of competitiveness in international trade was protection, and the US had shown the way in this regard (pp. 123–126).

Unlike other radical scholars, Emmanuel did not view foreign direct investment by MNCs as a mechanism of surplus extraction. In fact, he showed empirically that little capital flowed to non-oil producing underdeveloped countries making charges of surplus extraction moot (1976, pp. 758–760). He took radical scholars to task for an inconsistent position of criticizing MNCs for setting up enclaves with no linkages with the domestic economy while simultaneously blaming MNCs for undermining productive capacity in underdeveloped countries.

Based on the Marxist concept of developing productive forces, Emmanuel actually welcomed the possibility of technology transfer from MNCs. Low wages could actually be a deterrent since they resulted in a shallow market, but if a way around this problem was production for export, "it is rather a matter for rejoicing" (p. 766). Thus, technological progress was to be welcomed as a means of developing productive forces. In this regard, then, Emmanuel viewed appropriate or intermediate technology (see Schumacher, Chapter 5) as anti-development since it would relegate underdeveloped countries to backwardness (p. 764).[15] Ultimately, then, the problem was not that MNCs created dependency and underdevelopment, but rather that they engaged in too little FDI in underdeveloped countries.[16]

Emmanuel (1975, p. 84) argued that notwithstanding claims by dependency theorists (see Chapter 4) MNCs could be agents of development rather than underdevelopment. In fact, countries like Taiwan, Hong Kong, and Brazil had developed by working effectively with FDI. He argued that the dependency theorist response was to call this phenomenon "growth" and not development, since they had painted themselves into a corner by arguing that FDI could not induce development. Emmanuel's response was the more growth the better for underdeveloped countries (p. 87), notwithstanding his nod to ecological constraints (p. 66).

Samir Amin

In *Accumulation on a World Scale*, Amin (1974, p. 23) accepted Emmanuel's analysis of international trade in principle, seeing it as a mechanism for the transfer of surplus value from the periphery to the center. Yet Amin saw the conflict as one of class struggle in the context of the world system rather than as one between nations as Emmanuel did.[17] On one side of the conflict was the world bourgeoisie, which was based in the "center" (developed countries) but included partner elites in the "periphery" (underdeveloped countries).[18] On the other side was the world proletariat. In the periphery, the proletariat included the industrial wage workers, the peasants, and the surplus labor, all of whom were integrated into world markets. Understanding this conflict required an analysis of the social formations in the center and periphery (pp. 24–25).

The capitalist mode of production was prevalent in the center where the internal market was pivotal. The periphery was subjected to external markets, which facilitated primitive accumulation on a world scale based on the exploitation of the periphery by the center (pp. 37–38). This primitive accumulation on a world scale facilitated reproductive accumulation in the center. Amin considered two cases. Labor productivity was the same for the modern sector in the periphery and the center, but wages were much lower in the periphery, so trade represented a transfer of surplus value to the center, much as Emmanuel suggested. This was even more pronounced in the traditional sector since direct labor represented most of the value of the products (pp. 57–59). While the surplus transferred was not insignificant as a percentage of GDP in the center, it was a large portion of the combined periphery GDP (p. 59).

Amin differentiated his analysis of the center-periphery wage gap from Emmanuel's by emphasizing the different social formations in the center and periphery. The trend towards monopolies in the center ensured a resistance to a fall in prices. It also enabled a rise in wages, hence creating a labor aristocracy in the center.[19] While labor in the center continued to be exploited, the exploitation of the periphery proletariat was "much more violent" (p. 600). Unlike in the center, where most income was in the form of profits from expanded reproduction (reinvestment of savings), the predominant income in the periphery was in the form of rent drawn from agrarian-based exports to the center. The increased rents were spent on luxury imports and hence did not increase the domestic demand for labor. The excess labor supply in the periphery resulted from two mechanisms: first, from the initiation of agrarian capitalism which drove peasants off the land (p. 381); second, from the decimation of crafts due to global manufacturing.

Crafts in the periphery were bypassed, since food and materials continued to go abroad and so the sector became irrelevant to the economy. In developed countries, crafts were gradually displaced by local manufacturing that absorbed the labor released (pp. 151–152). Some in the crafts sector move back to cultivating their small plots but, because this type of cultivation was mostly for household consumption, Amin viewed this shift to be retrogressive in terms of the development of productive forces. Most of the surplus labor ended up in the informal sector (p. 157).

The main obstacle to articulated (non-distorted) industrialization in the periphery was the competition from the center. Such competition caused local commercial capitalists to invest their profits for land acquisition (p. 177). However, as production became more sophisticated in the center, and the "organic composition of labor increased," (the proportion of highly skilled workers grew in the labor force)[20] low wages drew capital to the periphery to start light industry. However, while local manufacturing was initiated, the borrowed technology was capital intensive and unable to absorb the labor surplus (pp. 151, 176).

Exporting capital from the center to the periphery served primarily to offset the falling rate of profit in the center (pp. 225–228). Amin argued that while some countries in the periphery might experience growth spurts, the transition to full-fledged, articulated, auto-centric (sustained) capitalist development for countries in the periphery was blocked by serving the needs of the center. This meant investing extensively in infrastructure and increasing imports of capital and intermediate goods, which led to recurring crises in public finance and balance of payment respectively. In this way, peripheral countries were held back. According to Amin, this explained why no country had moved from underdeveloped to developed status at the time of his writing in the 1970s (pp. 299–302).

In *Unequal Development* (1976), which covered much the same ground, Amin speculated that the East Asian countries hosting the light industry shifted out of the center were unlikely to "take-off" into auto-centric development. This prediction was premised on his observation of balance of payment problems, as well as structural weaknesses such as capital and technological dependency (p. 213). The periphery's balance of payment problems were compounded as capital flowed from the center to finance light capital industry, because this inflow was less than the backflow of profits to the center.

To sum up, relations with the center resulted in underdevelopment and distorted development in the periphery. Distorted development was characterized by export orientation to serve the needs of the center, a bias towards light industry, and the hypertrophy (expansion) of the tertiary sector as explained above (p. 288). Aid flows from the center enabled it to control the nature of development and perpetuate dependence (p. 247). Labor migration from the periphery was engineered to weaken the leverage of labor in the center and also represented a transfer of surplus from the periphery, which had invested in building labor skills. Thus, the only way to move out of underdevelopment and end distorted development was by breaking away from the world market or by severing relations with the center.

Bill Warren, 1935–1978

Warren (1973) took neo-Marxist and dependency theorists (see chapter 4) to task for being analytically and empirically wanting.[21] He questioned the validity of "widespread populist-liberal opinion" on the outcomes of colonialism and imperialism, producing a critique that was both distinctive and highly contested, coming as it did from a self-professed Marxist. He argued that underdeveloped countries, acting as a group or individually, used nationalist impulses to acquire considerable leverage in their dealings with developed countries and MNCs. They then used this leverage to ensure indigenous development of capitalism. (pp. 12–15).[22]

Essentially, the underdeveloped countries exploited Cold War rivalries. Similarly, they were able to exploit the rivalries among MNC subsidiaries. This leverage was evident in their ability to impose an oil embargo, nationalize MNC assets, forge independent trade and economic policies, and create institutions and organizations (like development banks) to engender local capitalism. Leverage was also evident in their ability to reduce MNCs' share of profits and rents in resource industries and engage in more resource processing locally (pp. 20–21).

Underdeveloped countries used their leverage over MNCs to indigenize manufacturing, acquire technology, and push manufactured exports (pp. 22–26). Moreover, while much of the impetus for capitalist development was indigenous, developed countries saw the spread of capitalism as a mechanism for containing social revolution and actually encouraged light and heavy manufacturing and made trade concessions (p. 15). Ultimately, this extension of capitalism to the non-capitalist world was undermining imperialism, "the international system of inequality and exploitation" (p. 41).

Warren developed these themes further in his book *Imperialism: Pioneer of Capitalism* (1980), which was published after his death and with significant editing by John Sender. In it, Warren argued that colonialism "was a powerful engine of progressive social change by destroying pre-capitalist social systems and implanting elements of capitalism" (p. 10). Warren saw his view in keeping with Marx's prediction. In contrast, he considered Lenin's analysis of imperialism (see Chapter 1) as self-serving propaganda for the Russian Revolution, not supported by evidence and contrary to fundamental Marxist precepts. Warren argued that Lenin's doctrine eliminated from Marxist scholarship the notion that capitalism could induce social and economic progress in pre-capitalist societies as it had done in Europe (p. 48).

According to Warren, this occurred because neo-Marxism equated Lenin's analysis of imperialist monopoly capitalism with neo-colonialism that they viewed as essentially destructive of underdeveloped societies and economies. As with colonialism, Warren regarded this view as contrary to the evidence and set out to empirically show that both colonialism and neo-colonialism were coeval with the enhancement of material wellbeing and the development of productive forces, first in the colonies and then in underdeveloped countries after independence.

Using logic and available evidence, he first argued the Marxian position that colonialism contributed to enhancing the education, health and sustaining consumption of the population, hence it indirectly contributed to improving the productive forces and directly to increasing material wellbeing (p. 129). By establishing communications and infrastructure colonialism directly contributed to productive forces and also virtually eliminated famines (p. 134). As local capitalism took root, crafts declined, but this was not necessarily a problem given that the opportunities presented by industrialization were superior to the "primitive economy yielding a primitive livelihood" (pp. 131–132). "Progressive imperialism" was conducive to the development of productive forces via three mechanisms. It transplanted Western techniques, culture and institutions to the less developed countries (LDCs), stimulated aspirations "in degree and kind," and displaced primitive modes of production (pp. 114, 136).

Warren further argued that in the wake of colonialism, underdeveloped societies and economies were enriched by continued contact with the West. He claimed that the concern about outflows of surplus being greater that inflows from FDI was mistaken because the surplus had to be created before division, and that once there was value added, some of that value would be locally retained. Thus, the drain of surplus was relative and not absolute, and therefore both sides of the transaction would inevitably benefit from FDI (p. 142).

If LDCs initially exported primary commodities this did not represent a structurally imposed international division of labor, but rather a sensible strategy to earn needed foreign exchange. Warren cited the counter-evidence to dispute the notion of a secular decline in the terms of trade for primary commodities (refer to en. 3, Chapter 4), and also provided evidence indicating a diversification into manufacturing based on nationalist impulses. In Warren's view, the expansion of industry was regretfully at the expense of agriculture and thus possible synergies between the sectors were lost (pp. 144–146, 226).[23]

Warren asserted that, contrary to the enclave production hypothesis, there was a rising share of manufactured exports, increased local content, forward and backward linkages, and local hiring in LDCs countries engaged with FDI. Assuming assembly in partnership with MNCs did not prevent diversification even into engineering goods (p. 179). Overall, there was not a great deal of FDI flowing to LDCs, but countries that were more engaged with FDI and manufactured exports, as were Taiwan and Korea, grew more (p. 184). He presented evidence to suggest that both light and heavy manufacturing output of LDCs grew more than twice as fast during 1971 to 1976 as that of developed countries and that this rate was a good deal above the normal average in developed countries.[24] This was not simply a reflection of the LDCs starting from a small base because the evidence suggested a sustained momentum, longer than any previously recorded (p. 241). The LDC market was not simply for elite luxury goods but consumer durables were diffused to the lower income urban groups (p. 247).

He argued that on balance the evidence with regard to the growth of material wellbeing was also positive. Growth rates in the LDCs' per capita GDP presented a more "cheerful picture" post-World War II, compared to the colonial period and also (with caveats) in comparison to the industrializing phase of the developed countries (pp. 190–199). He cited evidence to indicate that per capita GDP was associated with social indicators and hence "may not be a bad measure" of the pace of economic development. He denied that open unemployment rates were high or that there was much underemployment and argued that life in shanty towns was a marked improvement over village life (p. 228).

He cited evidence to suggest that caloric intakes were increasing, as were health and life expectancies, while educational attainment and housing were improving, and poverty was decreasing (pp. 231–232). He saw the increase in population growth rates as evidence that basic needs were being met (p. 235). He also made a case for trickle down (pp. 221–224), based on "mildly hopeful" evidence that growth and equity were not in conflict. He argued that in any case one could rule out the disastrous deterioration of income distribution brought on by growth as claimed (p. 204).[25]

To sum up, Warren's view was that capitalism was getting established in the Third World and contributing to the development of productive forces and material wellbeing, all contrary to the claims of neo-Marxist and dependency scholars. He acknowledged that LDCs were heterogeneous and so development by classes, regions, ethnic groups varied as expected and this posed a challenge to the national integration (p. 189). Bourgeois nationalism he believed was "a fundamental ideological condition for the creation of a modern nation state out of states previously characterized by feudal particularism, religious and communal division, and all manner of patriarchal backwardness" (p. 185).

He argued that neo-Marxism and dependency theory did these states a disservice by allowing them to externalize the blame for their own failings by placing the onus on "alleged enemies" (p. 59). As a Marxist, Warren welcomed capitalism since it would ultimately form the proletariat, which was the instrument for the creation of socialism (p. 25). Along the way, he argued that capitalism and social democracy went hand in hand and that capitalist societies contributed to the rights and the material wellbeing of the population very early on, since the inception of capitalism.

Summary and conclusions

Paul Baran was the pioneer for neo-Marxist thinking in development economics. He observed that colonialism had weakened the newly independent underdeveloped countries and that neo-colonialism exploited this weakness, allowing developed countries to extract surplus much as colonial countries had done. The instrument of this extraction was foreign direct investment (FDI) with multinational corporations (MNCs) as the vehicle. These companies were "aided and abetted" by the governments of the developed countries where they were based, using aid and technical assistance as leverage. Military aid and alliances were designed to ensure regimes remained friendly to the MNC objectives.

Baran also explained the persistence of underdevelopment in a way that to some extent still rings true: A regressive coalition of feudal and monopoly capitalists indulge in Veblen-like competitive luxury consumption, which dissipates the social surplus. Baran noted that social inequality and concentration of wealth created low effective demand, which represented a disincentive to mass production. Simultaneously, the fear of political instability and merchant-like preference for quick returns (a mentality born of colonialism) kept monopoly capitalists from engaging in long term socially productive investments.

Like developmentalists and Latin structuralists, Baran believed that economic development could be achieved through industrialization based on competitive capitalism. He saw industrialization as the only mechanism for modernizing agriculture by providing materials and machinery and absorbing the labor surplus released. Concomitantly, with the ensuing prosperity, effective demand would also be created for mass production. The path to development was straightforward. Progressive agrarian reform would unleash agrarian productive forces. Progressive taxation could be used to provide the physical and human capital that would crowd in businesses. Domestic capital accumulation would be encouraged through limits on luxury consumption and capital flight that might otherwise dissipate the surplus.

Although Baran's prescription was broadly similar to those advocated by the developmentalists or Latin structuralists, he was pessimistic about implementation. Unlike the developmentalist, Baran incorporated state theory into his analysis. He saw the state as representing feudal and monopoly capitalist interests, and it was unreasonable to expect the state to hurt these interests by taxing them to build a competitive capitalism that would threaten them further.

In his earlier work, Baran endorsed a social revolution and a collectivist economy (industrial planning and collective agriculture). But, perhaps due to his disillusion with the Soviet Union, his later work appeared to endorse competitive capitalism that would reward industry, ability and efficiency. This outcome would need to be attained with the support of the middle classes, which had traditionally aligned themselves with the retrogressive forces in order to share privileges. The alliance had been cemented by their mutual fear of a social revolution, which appeared on the horizon due to the post-World War II ideological competition. The question that Baran asked was whether the middle classes would play their historical progressive role as they had in the developed countries, or would they "commit suicide from fear of death?" (1973, p. 102).

With hindsight it is possible to see that the middle-classes were not the only ones capable of implementing the type of state-led development that Baran and the developmentalists endorsed. In fact, Baran himself noted that in East Asia, patriotic military regimes had adopted a state-led approach of promoting agrarian reform, blocking luxury consumption and capital flight (on pain of death), and investing in physical and human capital as the base for an elaborate industrial policy led development (see Chapter 7). A democratic process led by the middle classes, and one responsive to broad based constituencies, could ensure the diffusion of assets and power for inclusive development but this would be a much slower, even if less repressive, alternative.

Furtado extended class analysis to the Latin American context, specifically that of Brazil. He was more hopeful than Baran about the possibility that the national business elite might initiate internal capital accumulation and economic diversification. In Brazil, the class interests of the feudal elites favored overvaluation of the currency and this enabled the business class to build capacity. Furtado's state theory was also more complex and nuanced than Baran's; he saw the state as an arena for the contestation of conflicting class interests. Thus, he contested Baran's analysis, which implied a harmony of class interests among the ruling elites and their mutually beneficial alliance with foreign capital. Furtado also viewed national business as more capable of and keen to capture the domestic market. However, he foresaw that development was not assured and the system could stagnate into a rent-seeking low level equilibrium trap.

Furtado's deconstruction of effective demand represented a gloomy prognosis for small countries. He bifurcated effective demand into that pertaining to rich and poor consumers respectively. Among the feudal elite, average income increased from primary exports and they emulated the consumption patterns of elites in rich countries. In a large enough country, MNCs could realize scale economies and so extend production to a large underdeveloped economy to cater to this demand. Costs are low since no new technological development is required and modernization of agriculture yields surplus labor, which keeps wages low. There is also the hope of technological diffusion from MNCs, even though this would have to be despite MNC efforts to block access.

While poor consumers have a non-diversified, non-durable goods consumption basket, local industry may still realize scale economies by catering to this demand in a large country. Since small economies are unlikely to realize scale economies or external economies, and they face the on-going challenge of balance of trade deficits as the elite purchase imports to emulate foreign consumption patterns, local industrialization does not take root.

Arghiri Emmanuel challenged Ricardo's and other theories of comparative advantage by extending Marxian analysis to explore international trade. He explored what he viewed as the most realistic scenario consisting of immobile labor and mobile capital, which violated Ricardo's premise by suggesting equalization of profits but unequal wages. Emmanuel demonstrated that the wage structure within a country was determined by biological, historical, moral, social, political, and institutional (power relations) reasons and that the wage structure in developed countries was much higher than in underdeveloped countries. This unequal wage structure meant that international exchange was generally exploitative, with underdeveloped countries exchanging products that embodied more units of labor hours for products from developed countries that embodied far fewer unit hours of similarly skilled labor.

The solution, Emmanuel argued, was to limit unequal exchange via export taxes, subsidies for domestic diversification, and regional trade. Emmanuel distinguished international trade from FDI and had a favorable view of the latter in terms of the potential for technology transfer. In his view, the problem for underdeveloped countries was too little rather than too much FDI.

Samir Amin accepted Emmanuel's analysis regarding the transfer of surplus value from the periphery to the center, and his premise of unequal exchange arising from wage differentials. However, Amin suggested that the source of wage differential was rooted in the social formations in the center and periphery, hence he emphasized the centrality of historical materialism (see Chapter 2), which became a recurring theme in his work. In the center, the trend to monopolization explained the ability of firms to concede wage increases (creating a labor aristocracy) while resisting price decreases. In the periphery, the decimation of crafts by the import of products from the center created a pool of labor surplus that kept wages down. Capital flowed from the center to the periphery to avert the falling rate of profit in the center, and trade and capital flows also blocked development in the periphery. Breaking out of global trade was the mechanism to get out of underdevelopment. Amin's emphasis on capitalism as a world system that converted all labor in the periphery into an exploited proletariat and his additional emphasis on the agency of MNCs in bringing about this system distinguished his analysis from Emmanuel's.

Bill Warren viewed himself as an orthodox Marxist and was hostile to the neo-Marxism established by Baran and even more so to scholars of the dependency school (see Chapter 4). Marxism was the commonality between him and the other writers in this chapter in that they all endorsed the development of productive forces and the enhancement of material wellbeing, particularly for the proletariat. While the rest of the authors in this chapter thought that global capitalism hindered the development of productive forces in various ways, Warren used logic and available evidence to argue the Marxian position that contact with global capitalism, starting with colonialism, set the stage for the development of local capitalism by undermining primitive and retrogressive forces in underdeveloped areas

Colonialism, in his view, had made local populations materially better off compared to pre-colonial times, thanks to investments in social and physical infrastructure. Similarly, in the neo-colonial period global capitalism induced a discrete jump in the development of productive forces and material wellbeing across the board. He argued that nationalism, and the technology and learning offered by MNCs were central to this process.

In his text, he conceded that his survey of evidence was "inevitably impressionistic"; he identified appropriate caveats, but nonetheless found that there was much reason for optimism. In his conclusion he was less circumspect and stated that post-World War II there have been "titanic strides in the establishment, consolidation, and growth of capitalism in the Third World with corresponding advances in material welfare and the expansion of productive forces" (p. 252). He further remarked that this capitalism "has struck deep indigenous roots" and "manifests a rigorous internal momentum" (p. 253).

In setting up this thesis, Warren stated that obstacles to an even more robust development of capitalism were internal to Third World countries (p. 10). He elaborated on this claim, which became a theme in his text. While, as expected, there were variations in the spread of capitalism in the Third World, he wrote that the signs of progress in this regard were plentiful and widespread despite these internal obstacles.

History may well be on Warren's side regarding the spread of capitalism in the Third World and the concomitant growth of the proletariat, but the signs of the transition to socialism are not evident a half century after his controversial intervention. It is not clear that this would have mattered a great deal to Warren since another theme in his book is that capitalism and the social democracy that accompanied it enhanced rights and material wellbeing. That these appealing elements might have served as defensive measures for the capitalist system to protect itself, given the presence of a socialist alternative, might have been viewed as irrelevant by him. One can only speculate given that he did not have the opportunity to develop his scholarship.

Since history cannot be replayed, it is impossible to know for sure which of the two persuasive writers, Baran and Warren, was correct. Would productive forces in LICs and MICs have been at a more advanced stage currently if not disrupted by neo-colonialism, as Baran argued? Or did contact with progressive imperialism and neo-colonialism advance productive forces, as Warren believed? This is a question for continued historical speculation.

Notes

1 Baran recognized the many definitional difficulties associated with these concepts (p. 30).
2 This same phenomenon was later noted by neo-liberal economists in the 1970s as part of their critique of ISI (Chapter 6).
3 This is much like Alavi's (1972) concept of the state in post-colonial societies.
4 An extension of this model is that serving military leaders can play this dangerous game, and military elites often develop their own agenda and become a powerful faction of the ruling elite, if not the most powerful, no matter the class background from which the generals arose.
5 The Arab Spring suggests that in parts of the developing world this theory continues to have salience.
6 In appendix I of the book, Charles Bettelheim challenged Emmanuel for having deviated from orthodox Marxism in his analysis in several ways. Emmanuel contended that the working classes in underdeveloped countries are directly exploited by foreign capital in partnership with local elites through trade and also indirectly by the blocking of productive forces. Bettelheim argued that Emmanuel's analysis led him to the faulty conclusion that trade policy changes, rather than social revolution, could bring about substantive change. In appendices II and IV, Emmanuel defended his analysis for being correct and also Marxist though he conceded he was not orthodox.
7 For example, he argued that England possessed neither raw materials nor any weaving experience, except in wool, prior to establishing its cotton textile industry. Even the woolen industry was artificially implanted with draconian measures including cutting off the arms of any person who violated the ban on wool exports (p. 269).
8 Emmanuel (1975) revisited unequal exchange to develop some themes in his earlier works and also provided further evidence to back his theory including on the equalization of the rates of profit (pp. 51–54).
9 Emmanuel (1975) emphasized power relations between social classes in determining wages beyond some vital minimum. The higher the actual wages are relative to this minimum, the lower the ability of unions to deliver increases since they confront greater resistance from employers (pp. 47–50).
10 In this regard Emmanuel noted that Arthur Lewis got it right (refer to Chapter 2).
11 Emmanuel (1975, p. 67) suggested that it was inevitable for worker wages in developed countries to include surplus value drawn from the proletariat in underdeveloped countries. Thus he argued that international economic relations [trade] were the arena of the main contradiction in the Marxian sense.
12   Since diversification is risky and has a high gestation period, the state would need to support this activity with subsidies (p. 150).
13 In later work (1975, p. 78) Emmanuel defined development as the enhancement of productive forces and this was more consistent with the Marxist perspective. Ultimately, this reduced to labor productivity. He argued labor is perishable and hence distinct from the other factors, and knowledge, technology, and natural resources contribute in enabling it to enhance productive effort (p. 78). Capital accumulation and the effective use of the surplus, as happens in a capitalist economy and could do so in principle in a socialist economy, also enhanced labor productivity.

14 Emmanuel did not explicitly indicate that they also inherited Britain's institutional framework.
15 These themes are more fully developed in Emmanuel (1982).
16 He viewed production and technology to follow consumption and the strength and dominance of the US economy he considered was based on its ability to market (1975, pp. 71–72).
17 Amin (1977, pp. 216–223) asserted that his theory of unequal exchange, which led to unequal development, was theoretically sounder than Emmanuel's. He rejected Emmanuel's views of specificity of products, arguing that the center and periphery can and do produce the same products, and also of the association of wages to productivity. He also explored the associated transformation problem of the conversion of value into prices, an issue Emmanuel bypassed (pp. 223–225).
18 Wallerstein (1979), a sociologist, is another prominent world system theorist.
19 In Amin (1977, p. 222), he associated the wage differential to the differential in development of productive forces in the center and periphery, which, as a more general explanation, would subsume the specific explanations in the text.
20 Amin credited Emmanuel for this term.
21 Warren is included in this chapter because he critiqued neo-Marxism.
22 Emmanuel (1977) acknowledged that Warren's contribution was "very important" (p. 61) but challenged his interpretation of the evidence and pointed out that Warren had conceded that the flow of foreign capital to underdeveloped countries was minimal (p. 75).
23 As a Marxist he viewed land reform as possibly damaging and endorsed capitalist agriculture on a larger scale to enhance agricultural productivity (p. 226).
24 Warren emphasized that this growth took place during peace time while links between developed and underdeveloped countries were strong. This emphasis was to counter the view of neo-Marxists like Samir Amin or dependency theorists like Andre Gunder Frank that delinking is the only option for moving out of underdevelopment. Frank provided evidence of higher development during major wars when such links were weakened (see Chapter 4).
25 The reference in this paragraph is to the Kuznets curve (Kuznets, 1955) (also refer to Chapter 2).

References

Alavi, H. 1972. "The State in Post-Colonial Societies: Pakistan and Bangladesh." *New Left Review*, 74, 59–81.
Amin, S. 1977, *Imperialism and Unequal Development*. New York: Monthly Review Press.
Amin, S. 1976, *Unequal Development: An Essay on the Social Formations of Peripheral Capitalism*. New York: Monthly Review Press.
Amin, S. 1974. *Accumulation on a World Scale*. New York: Monthly Review Press.
Baran, P. 1973. "On the Political Economy of Backwardness." In: Charles K. Wilber, eds., *The Political Economy of Development and Underdevelopment*. New York: Random House.
Baran, P. 1957. *The Political Economy of Growth*. New York: Monthly Review Press.
Emmanuel, A. 1982. *Appropriate or Underdeveloped Technology?* Chichester: John Wiley & Sons.
Emmanuel, A. 1977. "Myth of Development vs. Myths of Underdevelopment." *New Left Review*, 85 (May–June), 61–82.
Emmanuel, A. 1976. "The multinational corporation and inequality of development." *International Social Science Journal*, 38 (4), 754–772.

Emmanuel, A. 1975. "Unequal Exchange Revisited." Institute of Development Studies Discussion Paper No. 77. University of Sussex. Brighton.

Emmanuel, A. 1972. *Unequal Exchange: A Study of Imperialism of Trade*. New York: Monthly Review Press.

Furtado, C. 1973. "The Brazilian Model of Development." In: Charles K. Wilber, eds., *The Political Economy of Development and Underdevelopment*. New York: Random House.

Furtado, C. 1964. *Development and Underdevelopment*. Los Angeles: University of California Press

Kuznets, S. 1955. "Economic Growth and Income Inequality." *American Economic Review,* 45 (1), 1–28.

Wallerstein, I. 1979. *The Capitalist World-Economy*. Cambridge: Cambridge University Press.

Warren, B. 1980. *Imperialism: Pioneer of Capitalism*. London: Verso.

Warren, B. 1973. "Imperialism and Capitalist Industrialization." *New Left Review*, 81 (September–October), 3–44.

4 Structuralism and dependency theory

Introduction

The structural thinkers discussed in this chapter, Raul Prebish, Hans Wolfgang Singer, and Gunnar Myrdal, share much with the developmentalists as far as their theories of underdevelopment were premised on structural factors.[1] However, their focus on external factors such as uneven development and asymmetrical power relations constitutes an important difference. This focus on the disadvantageous consequences of these external relations led the structuralists to doubt that underdeveloped countries could attain development as a result of trade and foreign investment.

Beyond endorsing the developmentalists prescriptions, structuralist authors appealed to developed countries to rectify trade and investment rules and to assist underdeveloped countries in addressing export instability and attaining endogenous technological growth. The combination of these prescriptions was referred to as the New Internal Economic Order, and this was promoted by some low income countries in the 1970s. Because the NIEO portrayed the current system of international trade as a zero-sum game, its prescriptions were rubbished by mainstream economists and did not gain traction in the West (Johnson, 1976).[2]

Partly as a response, a more radical strain of development thinking, called dependency theory, emerged from Latin America, and it focused on exploitative international links between developed and developing countries as a theory of underdevelopment. This analysis gained traction and was subsequently used by scholars in other parts of the developing world, particularly Africa.

Key thinkers

Structuralism

Raul Prebish (1901–1986)

Prebish was first to popularize the terminology of center (United States as the new principal Center, reconstructing European countries, Oceana, and Japan) and periphery (consisting of Latin American and other underdeveloped countries). In his classic *Economic Development of Latin America* (1950), Prebish's main concern was how the US, as the dominant center, impacted Latin American economic growth. US behavior was different from that of Great Britain, which had previously been the principal center. The US had both higher productivity and a lower import coefficient than Britain, which resulted in a scarcity of dollars. High productivity in the US also led to higher domestic wages, which inevitably made some US industries less competitive. But, unlike Britain, the US protected these industries. Various elements of this thesis were viewed as having broader relevance.

Much like the classical political economists and the developmentalists, Prebish recognized that the incidence of technical progress was greater in the industrial sector (concentrated in the center) than in primary goods production (in the periphery). More important and relevant to his thesis was his observation that the fruits of this technical progress were not evenly distributed across the rich industrial countries and the periphery (pp. 8–16). Economic logic would suggest that if there was greater technical change in the center than in the periphery, the terms of trade should move in favor of the periphery and the fruits of technical change would be passed on to the periphery through lower prices. Yet, Prebish cited evidence showing the terms of trade turned systematically against the periphery from 1876 to 1938 (Table 1, p. 9). Compared to the 1860s, only 63 percent of the finished manufactures could be bought in the 1930s with a given amount of primary products (p. 8).[3]

Prebish concluded that the rise in productivity that accompanied technical progress in the center was absorbed either by rising factor incomes or increased leisure (a shorter work week). Meanwhile, technical progress in the periphery was passed on in lower prices and hence the fruits of productivity gains were again primarily enjoyed by the center.[4] Even in business cycle downturns, wage rigidity in the center protected incomes, but it caused greater price pressure in the periphery. The lack of labor organization prevented workers in the periphery from protecting their income.

Following standard economic theory, Prebish asserted that economic growth requires enhancing productivity by increasing the capital labor ratio and acquiring techniques for the effective use of the capital and this would follow capital accumulation. Yet, when the terms of trade turn against primary products, the accumulation process became more challenging. He suggested that by mechanizing agriculture, and making it more efficient, trade would enable primary product exports to import the capital goods and the technology needed. In addition, the industrialization that would occur as a result would allow underdeveloped countries to capture the fruits of technical progress.

However, he made no unqualified endorsement of the import substitution industrialization (ISI) that Prebish became associated with. Rather, devaluations, higher tariffs, import quotas, and exchange controls were suggested as a defensive strategy, and for multiple reasons. First, they would enable underdeveloped countries to overcome the trade imbalances that resulted from the low import coefficient and protection in the US (p. 29). Second, given the dollar scarcity, these strategies were intended to ensure that there was sufficient foreign exchange to pay for the needed capital goods (p. 45). Third, the strategy could help avoid the shocks resulting from cyclical fluctuations in the center, although Prebish qualified this by pointing out that if production was not efficient, the unemployment costs of these fluctuations might be lower than the inefficiency costs (p. 53). Fourth, while luxury consumption could undermine the drive to enhance labor productivity by raising capital labor ratios, market intervention could contain such consumption (p. 5). Fifth, the same measures could help contain unemployment, important given that primary production would not absorb the entire labor force, especially given technical change.[5]

In modern parlance, Prebish could be viewed as a "liberal" economist. He welcomed foreign trade and foreign direct investment, but was concerned that these, along with foreign assistance, should work for Latin America. In keeping with this liberal outlook, he was concerned with efficiency and saw no sound economic reason for forcing the establishment of capital goods industries. Of course, if industrial development, technical skills and capital accumulation led underdeveloped countries in that direction, it would be welcome as "encouraging proof of maturity" (p. 58). Recognizing that there would be a move to intermediate and capital goods as industrialization based on production of consumer durables was exhausted, he recommended establishing a regional common market to facilitate this transition. His endorsement of planning was limited to complementing the private sector, partly by investment in infrastructure.

Prebish also proposed buffer stock programs for primary goods set up with international assistance as part of a win-win strategy to counter business cycles. During downturns, purchase of primary goods would limit the fall in aggregate demand for center products and at the same time limit the secular decline in the terms of trade against primary commodities (p. 57). This suggestion in particular stood out among those of his contributions that were incorporated into the platform for the New International Economic Order (NIEO).

Prebish also introduced an analysis of structural inflation based on the concept of social surplus left over after social reproduction (1984, pp. 185–190). He showed that growth required much of the social surplus to be devoted to investment, and this conflicted with the interests of labor, as well as of those of the upper class (wishing to funnel capital towards conspicuous consumption), and the state (needing funds to accommodate surplus manpower and a growing bureaucratic empire). Also, oligopolistic transnational corporations internationalized consumption and siphoned off a disproportionate share of the surplus. Structural inflation resulted when monetary authorities, seeking to ensure social stability, attempted to accommodate these competing claims. Prebish found it ironic that economic liberals recommended wage repression to curb inflation (central also to later structural adjustment programs – see Chapter 6) since this entailed curbing political liberalism.

Essentially, his prescriptions called for drawing on the best of socialism and the market system, which together amounted to a form of social democracy. He also urged high income countries to engage in multi-lateral trade liberalizations that would extend to commodities in which underdeveloped countries had a comparative advantage. These liberalizations had not happened in the GATT (General Agreement on Trade and Tariffs) Kennedy or Tokyo Rounds and hence they became another element in the call for a NIEO.

After producing his analysis of structural inflation, Prebish took over the directorship of the CEPAL Review. His articles (1976, 1978, 1980, 1981) for the journal explored his concerns with internal and external power asymmetries and their impact on the economy. His writings were concerned with the "primary" and "secondary" appropriation of surplus by the upper and middle strata to the exclusion of the lower strata, and with the role of multinational corporations in international development. In particular, he focused on the fact that they failed to promote indigenous technological acquisition and learning, and instead promoted an imitative consumer society, thus distorting development and enabling surplus to be syphoned off to the center.

Hans Wolfgang Singer (1920–2006)

Singer was a German born economist who studied issues similar to those studied by Prebish; although working independently, Singer came to similar conclusions. He viewed much of primary export production in underdeveloped countries in the 1950s as the product of foreign investment driven by multinationals (1964, pp. 163–164). Although export production occurred within underdeveloped countries, it was not part of the domestic economic structure; in fact, the secondary multiplier effects of such production accrued abroad because foreign firms repatriated profits. He argued that the opportunity of putting the royalties to good use by underdeveloped countries was for the most part missed.

Singer also observed that in the long term, prices moved against primary goods. He ruled out the possibility that this was the consequence of higher productivity in the primary sector (1964, p. 166). Instead, he explained this decline in terms of low income elasticity of demand for primary goods, high income elasticity of demand for manufactured goods, and low wages associated with surplus labor in underdeveloped countries (1984, p. 291). Another important factor was the level of technical progress in developed countries, which resulted in substitutes for primary goods and economies in their use and therefore decreased the need to import them. Singer pointed out that price inelastic demand for primary products resulted in large revenue losses when business cycles reduced demand in developed countries.

He argued that a move to manufacturing was desirable because it would result in higher levels of education, inventiveness, and technical change, creating more demand and Marshallian externalities. Manufacturing was "a central factor of dynamic radiation which has revolutionized society in the industrialized countries." Yet underdeveloped countries suffered because manufacturing had been "withheld from the course of their economic history." Singer's prescription was for a more fluid international division of labor that would allow for more extensive industrialization within underdeveloped countries. He argued that the structure of comparative advantages and countries' relative endowments at a given point in time should not determine the future division of labor (p. 172).[6]

In a follow-up work co-authored with Ansari (1977, pp. 36–37), Singer argued that unequal relations between developed and developing countries were more critical in price determination than unequal outcomes that are likely from product specialization. In a retrospective on his own thought, Singer (1984, p. 283) pointed out that the debate really needed to be cast in terms of developed and developing countries rather than commodities, and credited Charles P. Kindleberger with having correctly cast the debate in terms of country groups and with having found that the terms of trade moved in favor of the developed countries over time.[7]

Singer and Ansari argued that modern technology, rather than product specialization, was the main advantage of developed economies. Developed countries were the base for the MNCs that housed this important technology. In order for poor countries to attain prosperity and remove technological dependence, they needed to adopt and adapt, and develop an indigenous technological capacity suited to their needs. The successful late industrializers were the ones that managed to facilitate technological development by creating the necessary institutions. Thus, international assistance in the form of grants, technological assistance and trade concessions would need to facilitate institution building in order to help develop poor countries (p. 40). A priori, it would not seem to be in the interest of the developed countries to undermine their advantage by facilitating catch up, but Singer and Ansari suggested that a more prosperous world would be in everyone's long term interest.

Reflecting on obstacles poor countries confronted they pointed to the adverse impact of market power exercised by MNCs, export instability, tariff barriers, tariff escalation and non-tariff barriers imposed on developing country exports (pp. 74–80).[8] They calculated that in 1972 the effective rates of protection (ERP) that developed countries imposed against imports from underdeveloped countries were 109 percent higher than on imports from other developed countries.

Gunnar Myrdal (1898–1987)

Myrdal could well be classified as a developmentalist or institutionalist: he believed in endemic market failures in underdeveloped countries and strongly advocated development planning (1970). But while the theory of circular cumulative causation that he developed could explain regional inequality within countries, Myrdal (1957) used it to address his key research question of global divergence. His unique contribution to development economics thinking derived from focusing on the structure of the international economy and he used this to explain the very large and rising inequalities between poor and rich countries.

Myrdal started by establishing value premises, arguing that development should be measured in terms of improvements in equality of opportunity and political democracy (pp. 9–10). He viewed the two values as being intricately related: he associated mass poverty in underdeveloped countries with a lack of equality of opportunity, a condition which failed to produce and nourish political democracy.

Myrdal viewed equilibrium analysis as irrelevant for a sound theory of under-development or development. (pp. 74–80). Vicious or virtuous circles were embedded in his theory of circular cumulative causation and these led away from the initial point when no countervailing market forces pushed back to the initial point. (p. 13). In fact, in the case of regional inequality, Myrdal argued that market forces would exaggerate the trend of divergence from the initial point.

Suppose one region thrives due to historical accident, resource concentration, or geographical advantage. Internal and external economies would make this region a magnet for resources as the market mechanism acted to draw in human and financial capital from other regions, exemplifying a virtuous circle (pp. 26–27). This play of market forces, however, would also set into motion vicious circles in regions from which resources were drawn. In these regions, the demographics would become unfavorable, the market size would shrink and their handicrafts and industries would be wiped out unable to compete with the nodal centers (growth poles) experiencing increasing returns.

Thus, the process of cumulative causation could be simultaneously positive and negative. Myrdal referred to the negative impacts on the deprived regions as "backwash effects." But, these negative effects were balanced with a counter-vailing market mechanism that he referred to as a "spread effect." He argued that since growth poles would in due course become markets for materials and products from other regions, this would allow self-sustained economic prosperity to spread out into peripheral areas. Myrdal noted that in the more prosperous coun-tries, the state offsets backwash effects and facilitates spread effects by funding social and physical infrastructure. Investing in people's education and health makes them more productive and allows their potential to be realized. This enables prosperity to be generalized and facilitates attaining national integration (p. 31). In this way, social equality serves as a mechanism for economic growth.

Myrdal disputed the existence of any pure price or market mechanism since it functions within an institutionalized context where prices are influenced by taxes and regulations (p. 48). Hence, the price mechanism could be viewed as a servant to the public interest rather than a master (p. 80). Particularly in a demo-cracy, the political process could preserve this role for the market by preventing vested interests from capturing the state and controlling the price mechanism. Poorer countries, however, lacked resources to facilitate spread effects and also lacked the political structure to prevent the state from being captured. These dif-ferences could explain regional inequality and underdevelopment (pp. 42–43).[9]

The same forces of circular cumulative causation that induce regional inequality within countries enhance global inequalities. Advanced country manufactured goods wipe out craft and manufacturing products if protection is not provided (p. 52). As suggested by Prebish and Singer, inelastic demand, price fluctuations and low potential for technological learning are forthcoming from specializing in primary goods as recommended by rich country economists espousing comparative advantage (p. 53).[10] Another backwash effect is capital outflows to the richer coun-tries if not constrained (p. 54). While theory suggests a higher return to capital where it is scarce, without state support the returns to capital are low and insecure.

In the relations between rich and poor nations, there is no global governance and hence no one to impose countervailing spread effects. Based on national interest, the initiatives within the UN to restrain capital outflows and make global trade rules fairer via price stabilization mechanisms and competition policies to offset international cartels were undermined by the developed countries (p. 73). Similarly, technical assistance was nominal and aid was a mechanism for promoting the national interests of donor countries (p. 71).[11]

Like Marx (see Chapter 1), Myrdal believed that colonialism, although primarily self-serving, also did some good for the colonized countries. Infrastructure, institutions of law and order, a civil service, elementary sanitation, and education all set the stage for later development (p. 56). However, "enforced bilateralism" imposed a high cost in terms of opportunities foregone that could have resulted from relations with other countries (p. 58). Segregation in enclave primary production limited the transfer of technical skills and entrepreneurial ability (p. 58). The interests of the privileged classes, that were co-opted, hardened institutions of inequality such as a semi-feudal and a caste or ethnicity based order that offset spread effects even after independence. (p. 60). He argued that for the most part the "civilizing mission and other associated phraseologies were largely rationalization of economic interests" (p. 61).

Myrdal's theory of development was premised on struggle. He claimed that even in rich countries, rights, privileges, and opportunities were hard earned rather than willingly conceded, belying the limits of a social philosophy with roots in the "enlightenment" (p. 68). Thus, poor countries, too, would need to struggle for greater prosperity, as would the poor within these poor countries. Landlords will not hand over their land to land-hungry peasants even if there is an economic productivity case for it and even if shattering the old class structure would enable spread effects (p. 68). Moreover, because rights in the richer countries are often won at the expense of the poor in poor countries, such as subsidies for cotton farmers, so underdeveloped countries need solidarity in international forums to resist this (p. 69).

Underdeveloped countries that seek prosperity, regional equality and national integration would need to use state planning to facilitate spread effects. (p. 80). Like other developmentalists, then, Myrdal viewed planning primarily as a mechanism to create space for markets by addressing rigidities and bottlenecks, which would in turn facilitate spread effects (pp. 81, 92). In relations with the developed nations, he advocated protection for "infant economies" until they thrived and produced dynamic social gains through the process of positive circular cumulative causation (p. 87).

Dependency

Andre Gunder Frank (1929–2005)

Prebish, Singer and Myrdal pointed to power asymmetries within the global economy, and suggested that this resulted in a raw deal for underdeveloped countries, but nonetheless hoped for a solution with in the world capitalist system. Yet they also set the stage for scholars like Frank, who were much less hopeful of a resolution within the world capitalist system and who implied that development could only be achieved by delinking from this system.[12] In his classic article on the development of underdevelopment, Frank asserted that this theory and its corollaries had been established in historical research by him (Frank, 1967), and by other scholars.[13]

Frank's argument was that underdevelopment could only be understood by studying the unique social and economic history of each underdeveloped country. Only then would it be possible to formulate an adequate theory of development (p. 103). In contrast to Rostow's grand theory with its broad brush historical formulations, Frank's approach purported to be country specific. Frank refuted Rostow's presumption that there are significant similarities between currently developed and underdeveloped countries in terms of their respective histories. He conceded that developed countries were at one point *un*developed, but pointed out that they had never been *under*developed, since the latter condition is an outcome of the colonialism, which developed countries were never subject to (p. 104).

Even though Frank's work suggested the importance of national and historical specificity, as a theorist he naturally made generalizations. His research was based on Latin American experience but the examples he used indicated that he intended his hypotheses to apply more generally to all relations between metropoles (center) and colonial (or post-colonial) societies (periphery).

Frank rejected Lewis' model of economic dualism (see Chapter 2) because Lewis's theory, like Rostow's, suggested that contact with the metropolis was necessary in order for underdeveloped countries to develop their modern sector instead of remaining in a subsistence based, pre-capitalist or feudal state. Frank himself contended that exposure to the metropolis is the cause of underdevelopment. He pointed out that the world capitalist system generally reached even the remotest part of underdeveloped countries and incorporated them in a nexus of surplus extraction (p. 104). The intensity of contact with the metropolis was proportional to the extent of underdevelopment within the exploited region. Thus, development could not follow from simply adopting the institutions and values of the currently advanced countries. Instead, as suggested by Singer and others, development would need to be based on an indigenous industrialization process that was "self-generating and self-perpetuating" (p. 106).

His first hypothesis was that relations between the metropolis and colonial countries, taking place within a global capitalist system, simultaneously generated development in the metropolis and underdevelopment in the satellites.[14] The exploitative relationship between the metropolis and the satellites was replicated within the satellite countries such that the national and regional capitals had a similarly exploitative relationship with the hinterland. This created a conveyor belt system whereby part of the surplus generated in remote outposts was transferred on to the regional or provincial cities and then on to the capital or economically dominant cities and then on to the metropolis (p. 5). In Frank's model, foreign investment in primary commodity production and exports were the mechanisms for this surplus transfer.[15]

His second hypothesis, which followed logically from the first, is that satellites experienced their greatest endogenous economic development when their ties with the metropolitan developed countries were severed or weakened, such as by wars or depressions. Similarly, any part of a country's hinterland that was somehow isolated from the world capitalist system would be more likely to experience development. Insulated from international investment and trade, these regions were able to nurture their manufacturing and perhaps even export, usually textiles. Applying this idea more broadly, Frank posited that Japan's success after the Meiji period was due to its non-satellite status (p. 109). It escaped the usual pattern of the destruction of manufacturing by international competition and lands appropriated and concentrated into *latifundia* or feudal estates for the "rapaciously growing export economy" concentrating on primary goods (p. 110).

Similar to his second hypothesis, Frank's third hypothesis was that the most feudal and underdeveloped countries were those that had once had the closest ties with the metropolis. Frank noted that these regions were often the primary good exporters and when demand declined they were abandoned (p. 110). The fourth hypothesis was that *latifundia* were part of the world capitalist system, and not vestiges of the feudal institutions once present in the metropolises. Rather, *latifundia* were born of commercial enterprise and created oppressive institutions to enable them to respond to world demand for primary goods. (p. 111). The fifth hypothesis was that those *latifundia* which did appear isolated, subsistence based and semi-feudal were only so because they had withered in response to a drop in world demand (p. 111). All in all, it was commercial rather than industrial capital that drove economic activity as part of the world capitalist system and accounted for the development of underdevelopment and in the "underdevelopment of development" (p. 112).

Fernando Henrique Cardoso and Enzo Faletto (1935–2003)

Cardoso and Faletto (1978) demonstrated the complexity of Latin American politics and social change in a historical narrative. They also explored dependency in the form of enclave production and subsequently dependent development post-World War II, after the nationalist and populist period of import substitution industrialization. While the version of the book drawn on here was translated in 1978, their research was conducted between 1965 and 1967.

Enclave production emerged as the nationally controlled economic sectors of commodity production were out-competed by more sophisticated technology and marketing systems requiring heavy capital investment. They also emerged as a direct result of the expansion of the center. In either case, local producers were precluded from developing an autonomous system of resource allocation (p. 70). The financial and commercial control of European capitalism (see Frank above) was oriented to controlling production in the peripheral world. The US was dominant in Latin America and success was premised on exports that generated large surpluses. Income was concentrated and therefore domestic demand was limited; another advantage of this mode of production for MNCs was that it did not require an internal market (p. 71).

The plantation enclaves were labor intensive while the mining enclaves were capital intensive but both resulted in a skewing of the income distribution. The mining enclave had high worker productivity because of the capital intensity and hence high worker wages but few links to the domestic economy. The plantation enclaves expanded at the expense of subsistence agriculture (p. 71). The strength of the plantation and mine owners depended on export success as earlier indicated. Local power brokers negotiated with the center externally and with the oligarchic dominant sectors internally on the terms that would be nationally acceptable for the economic exploitation of the enclaves. A control of at least part of local production and political unity enabled a more aggressive policy with regards to seeking tax concessions and compulsory reinvestment. The nationally dominant classes were oriented towards regulatory, political, and administrative state activities with a bureaucracy supported by taxes collected from the enclave sector (p. 72).

Industrialization associated with depended development relied on foreign investment. The dependency resulted from the need to withstand competition from multinationals with a large stock of technological knowledge and highly skilled managerial organization that could manage large scale production and quality control. In turn, capital flows and economic decisions such as profit reinvestment were controlled from abroad. Such dependent industrialization was substantially different from enclave economies since a highly diversified output was needed and reinvestment, especially in the capital goods sector, meant low profit repatriation. Further, these economies needed a tertiary sector and a more balanced income distribution to enable a domestic market to absorb output (pp. 162–163). Some Latin American economies like Brazil and Mexico were able to retain a degree of autonomy with the involvement of the public sector in production (p. 163).

The subordination by this monopolistic sector of other groups like workers, traditional agricultural interests, and displaced indigenous producers played out in the politics. The army and bureaucracy played a central role in the production system reorganization shifting the state from democratic and representative to authoritarian and corporatist (pp. 164–167). However, tensions remained between the older more national and equitable model of development, with the multinational corporation dominated model of dependent development and Cardoso and Felleto predicted that the outcome would be determined by the relative strength of the two forces. They also foresaw in the mid-1960s the space for autonomous development increasing as the world rebalanced due to a diffusion of power (especially the economic strength of Germany and Japan and the emergence of China as a political force) and hence the relative weakening of US hegemony. While multinational corporations continued to rely on US power to protect their interests, they also started making their own accommodations with changing economic realities that they partly ushered in (p. 171).

Summary and conclusions

Prebish's concern was that improved productivity in the center was internalized and resulted in more leisure or greater wages, whereas the fruits of any technical progress that occurred in the periphery were passed on to the center in the form of lower prices; thus the periphery could never reap the benefits of improved productivity. Economic logic would suggest that technical change in center products should result in lower prices and he cited evidence to show that, to the contrary, there was a secular increase in the terms of trade in center goods relative to the primary goods produced by the periphery. Institutional conditions such as the missing or weak labor unions in the periphery partly accounted for this. He encouraged industrialization in the periphery as part of the strategy to retain the fruits of its technical progress. In addition, he advocated mechanization as a way to increase productivity in agriculture and to ensure that profits from primary exports could be used to purchase the technology and capital goods that were needed for industrialization. He argued that, at first, purchasing capital goods would be more efficient than producing them domestically, and was thus preferable. Later, as the periphery acquired the ability to diversify and move up the value chain, capital goods could be produced within a regional common market, which he advocated as a way of achieving economies of scale.

Prebish's work became the foundation of the demand by underdeveloped countries for a New International Economic Order (NIEO) that would encompass fairer rules governing foreign trade and investment. In addition, he argued for a buffer stock mechanism for primary goods as a win–win strategy to both protect aggregate demand for the center's goods during recessions and to counter the secular decline in the periphery's terms of trade.

He proffered that inflation in Latin America had structural underpinnings, stemming from attempts by the monetary authorities to satisfy multiple groups with claims on the social surplus, including elites, oligopolistic multinationals, labor, and the expanding political machine. The accommodation of these demands was needed to avert social instability, but resulted in break-away inflation.

Like Prebish, Singer was pessimistic about the prospects of foreign trade and investment bringing about development in underdeveloped countries, though he was hopeful that foreign aid of the right kind might help. Asymmetrical power relations emerged as his main concern, and he demonstrated how these applied within a country just as they did across countries. Within countries, the rural sector was often disadvantaged in this regard. Internationally, underdeveloped countries were disadvantaged by a secular decline in the terms of trade. Among the reasons for this decline, Singer noted that MNCs sought to maximize profits at the expense of underdeveloped countries and that developed countries used their leverage to rig trade rules for their own benefit.

Though Singer came to believe that the key issue was power relations rather than product specialization, he was no different from other developmentalists in concluding that manufacturing was an inherently superior productive activity than primary goods production. He noted that manufacturing would result in various dynamic efficiencies, scale economies, higher productivity and Marshallian externalities. These benefits could not be achieved if comparative advantage remained the basis for product selection. Developing an indigenous technological capacity was critical for all underdeveloped countries, and it was imperative to create institutions that would facilitate this process. Foreign assistance, Singer believed, could be successful if applied to this endeavor.

In his early theorizing on circular cumulative causation Myrdal recognized the reality of uneven development resulting from backwash effects in relations between advanced and underdeveloped countries and identified trade and capital flows as the mechanisms exacerbating global inequalities in this regard. In his retrospective (1984, pp. 164–165) he focused on poor governance and urged that internal reforms should be the focus of attention. In a nutshell, he urged underdeveloped countries to heal themselves and took a dim view of the NIEO as unclear in its demands and as a smokescreen to externalize blame that should fall to bad leadership. [16]

Frank squarely placed the blame for underdevelopment on colonialism and subsequently on the role of post-colonial societies as satellites of the metropolitan centers of the global capitalist system. A pre-condition for the development of the metropolis was the underdevelopment of the satellites, while investment and trade were mechanisms for extracting surplus from those satellites. The commercial capital that drove the extraction process encouraged primary production for exports, promoting the establishment of *latifundia* (feudal estates) as a way of achieving more efficient extraction. Thus poor countries were unlikely to advance unless their ties with the metropolis were weakened, freeing them to advance towards self-generating and self-sustaining industrialization. As for Samir Amin (Chapter 3), the policy suggestion emerging from Frank's analysis was that countries must delink from the global capitalist system to industrialize. Contrary to his predictions, however, some underdeveloped countries later proved that engaging with the world capitalist system could be part of a successful development strategy; this was also pointed out by Warren (Chapter 3) and consistent with the view of other dependency scholars like Cardoso and Felleto.[17]

Cardoso and Felleto explained the nature of enclave production and dependent development emerging from foreign competition, interests and economic interventions. However, the alteration of domestic modes of production and how this played out in national politics was an important part of their narrative. They foresaw a growing space for autonomous development as economic and political power in the world was diffused by the emergence of new global players like Germany and Japan and the emergence of China and the subsequent lessening of US hegemony.

Notes

1 Toye (2005, pp. 126–127) attributed the origin of structuralist thinking to Michal Kelecki.
2 Refer to ed. Bhagwati (1977) for a more serious mainstream attempt to grapple with the issues involved. For a review of the NIEO refer to Dag Hammarskjöld Foundation (1975).

3 This finding sparked a statistical debate on whether this was actually the case. Prominent critics included Ellsworth (1956), Sparos (1980) and Michaely (1980) but support for the hypothesis persisted although it was reframed in terms of country groups rather than commodities once country data became available. With nuances, support for the long term secular decline in the barter terms of trade for underdeveloped countries right up to the turn of the twenty-first century is provided by Sarkar (2001), Ocampo (2010) and Bilge (2011).

4 In later work (1984) Prebish mentioned low inelasticity of demand for primary commodities relative to manufactured goods as another cause for the secular decline in the terms of trade. Market power of transnational corporations, he argued, also contributed to this phenomenon.

5 It was surprising then that Prebish declared himself, without qualification, to have been converted to protectionism during the inter-war years in a retrospective on his contributions to development thought (1984, p. 178).

6 This concept was later referred to as dynamic comparative advantage (see Chapter 7).

7 Singer (1984, pp. 284) also recognized that due the lack of data that subsequently became available, he was unable to weight barter terms of trade with respective factor productivities to estimate factoral terms of trade. However, since manufactured goods produced by developed countries were likely to experience greater productivity growth his estimates actually underestimated the extent of the decline in the terms of trade confronted by underdeveloped countries over time.

8 They cite a GATT report that listed 800 non-tariff barriers including quantitative restrictions, procurement procedures, standards, and custom regulations (p. 80).

9 In *The Asian Drama* (1968) and *The Challenge of World Poverty* (1970, chapter 4) negative cumulative causation within underdeveloped countries is also associated with the concept of a poorly managed "soft state" (unlike the developed country hard states) dominated by self-serving and corrupt elites who were above the law and hence incapable of inspiring social discipline.

10 Myrdal viewed the predictions of the Heckscher-Ohlin factors proportion trade model, particularly factor price equalization, to have been falsified by reality (pp. 148–149).

11 In *An International Economy* (1956, p. 124), Myrdal made a case for international aid to be multi-lateral to remove the political element from it.

12 Refer to Kay (1989) for a review of Latin American theories of development and underdevelopment. Kay thought that writers like Frank who wrote in English got disproportionate attention for their contributions to dependency analysis and sought to redress this imbalance in his book.

13 Frank used the inductive method and used case studies to establish his hypotheses. These may be considered patchy and not likely to meet the test of modern rigorous econometric evidence in terms of having established causality. However, impressive as the latter evidence appears, the edifice driving the empirical testing is often built on weak foundations (questionable premises and assumptions, faulty research design and sampling, and poor data).

14 Acemoglu and Robinson (2012) provide much support for Frank's various hypotheses in their chapters pertaining to colonialism, particularly chapter 9.

15 The accumulation processes that Myrdal described fit in well with Frank's theory, although Frank's explanation for regional inequality differed from Myrdal's circular negative cumulative causation in that he attributed the initial inequality to external intervention. Also, for Mrydal the market drove regional and global inequality while for Frank it was an engineered process.

16 Myrdal (1956, chapter 13) had earlier been supportive of the NIEO.

17 Frank is regarded by some to be a neo-Marxist scholar. On the left, however, he was critiqued for his focus on external links to the exclusion of class struggle and the internal modes of production as explanations for underdevelopment, charges that he acknowledged the validity of (1979a, p. xii).

References

Acemoglu, D. and Robinson J. A. 2012. *The Origins of Power, Prosperity, and Poverty: Why Nations Fail*. New York: Crown Business.

Bhagwati, J., ed., 1977. *The New International Economic Order: The North-South Debate*. Cambridge, Massachusetts: The MIT Press.

Bilge, E. 2011. "North-South Terms-of-Trade from 1960 to 2006." *International Review of Applied Economics*, 25 (2), 171–84.

Cardoso, F. H. and Faletto, E. 1978. *Dependency and Development in Latin America*, Translated by M. M. Urguidi. Berkeley: University of California Press.

Dag Hammarskjöld Foundation. 1975. "Towards a New International Order." In: *What Now: Another Development*. Prepared on the Occasion of the Seventh Special Session of the United Nations General Assembly, New York, 1–12 September 1975, Uppsala, Sweden.

Ellsworth, P. T. 1956. "The Terms of Trade between Primary Producing and Industrial Countries." *Inter-American Economic Affairs*, 10 (1), 47–65.

Frank, A. G. 1979a. *Dependent Accumulation and Underdevelopment*. New York: Monthly Review Press.

Frank, A. G. 1979b. "The Development of Underdevelopment." In: C. K. Wilber, ed., *The Political Economy of Development*. New York: Random House.

Frank, A. G. 1967. *Capitalism and Underdevelopment in Latin America: Historical Studies of Chile and Brazil*. New York: Monthly Review Press.

Johnson, G. H. 1976. "The New International Economic Order." Woodwart Court Lecture, University of Chicago, Booth School, Occasional Papers No. 49, Chicago, www.chicagobooth.edu/faculty/selectedpapers/sp49.pdf

Kay, C. 1989. *Latin American Theories of Development and Underdevelopment*. London: Routledge.

Michaely, M. 1980. "The Terms of Trade between Poor and Rich Nations." Vol. 162, Institute of International Studies, University of Stockholm.

Myrdal, G. 1984. "International Inequality and Foreign Aid in Retrospect." In G. M. Meier and D. Seers, eds., *Pioneers in Development*. New York: Oxford University Press.

Myrdal, G. 1970. *The Challenge of World Poverty: A World Anti-Poverty Program in Outline*. New York: Pantheon Books.

Myrdal, G. 1968. *Asian Drama: An Inquiry into the Poverty of Nations*. New York: Twentieth Century Fund and Pantheon Books.

Myrdal, G. 1957. *Economic Theory and Under-developed Regions*. London: Gerald Duckworth & Co., Ltd.

Myrdal, G. 1956. *An International Economy*. New York: Harper & Brothers Publishers.

Ocampo, J. A. 2010. "The Terms of Trade for Commodities since the Mid-19th Century." *Revista de Historia Economica*, 28 (1), 11–43.

Prebish, R. 1984. "Five Stages of My Thinking on Development." In: G. M. Meier and D. Seers, eds., *Pioneers in Development*. New York: Oxford University Press.

Prebish, R. 1981. "The Latin American Periphery in the Global System of Captialism." CEPAL Review, April 1981.

Prebish, R. 1980. "Towards a Theory of Change." CEPAL Review, April 1980.

Prebish, R. 1978. "Socio-Economic Structure and the Crisis of Peripheral Capitalism." CEPAL Review, second half of 1978.

Prebish, R. 1976. "A Critique of Peripheral Capitalism." CEPAL REVIEW, first half of 1976.

Prebish, R. 1950. *The Economic Development of Latin America and its Principal Problems.* Lake Success, New York: United Nations Department of Economic Affairs.

Sarkar, P. 2001. "The North-South Terms of Trade Debate: A Re-examination." *Progress in Development Studies*, 1 (4), 309–327.

Singer, H. W. 1984. "The Terms of Trade Controversy and the Evolution of Soft Financing." In: G. M. Meier and D. Seers, eds., *Pioneers in Development.* New York: Oxford University Press.

Singer, H. W. and Ansari, J. A. 1977. *Rich and Poor Countries.* Baltimore: The Johns Hopkins University Press.

Singer, H. W. 1964. *International Development: Growth and Change.* New York: McGraw-Hill.

Sparos, J. 1980. "The Statistical Debate between Primary Commodities and Manufactures." *Economic Journal*, (90), 107–28.

Toye, J. 2005. "The Significance of Keynes for Development Economics." In: Jumo, K. S., ed., *The Pioneers of Development Economics: Great Economists on Development.* New Delhi/London: Tulika Books/Zed Books.

Part II

Heterodox challenges from within the fold

5 Market-friendly heterodox approaches

Introduction

The authors reviewed in Chapter 3 and some in Chapter 4 challenged the dominant paradigm of neo-classical economics and the associated capitalist market system and proposed some form of socialist alternative. The heterodox authors or approaches reviewed in this chapter identify limitations of neo-classical economics as an adequate framework for understanding development. In addition, some of the authors in this chapter critique the development outcomes of a predominantly market based approach, particularly with regards to delivering social justice. Nonetheless, all the approaches reviewed in this chapter are within the market paradigm.

Douglass North as an institutional economist is difficult to classify and does not fit in neatly with the other approaches reviewed in this chapter. But, like all the authors in this chapter, his approach views institutions and institutional change as necessary for attaining identified objectives. The fundamental commonality among the other authors discussed in this chapter is their concern with social justice as a fundamental human need. Another commonality is that they are difficult to classify neatly into micro or macro. While they emerge from a micro focus, all advocate a macro scaling up.

As indicated, all these approaches advocate change from within the system and, as such, can be viewed as market friendly. However, they define parameters (social, political or ecological) within which markets should operate. These approaches include basic human needs, human development, gender and development, participatory development, and sustainable development. Participatory development differs from the other approaches in that, while it focuses on meeting basic needs, it provides an alternative mechanism for the realization of these needs than state and/or markets. Sustainable development is a broad approach that incorporates the focus and mechanisms of the others along with an ecological dimension. The common themes in these approaches include gender equality, employment, ecology, asset distribution and land reform, participation, and international aid.

Thinkers and approaches

Institutions and development: Douglass North[1]

Douglass North has written extensively on institutions, economic change and growth (1990, 2003, 2005). His earlier work developed conceptual building blocks for later work in which theories are honed and even modified as he himself suggests. I have therefore relied much more heavily on this later work that pertains to development economics.

North speculates on the big questions such as why and how some societies grew when they did and why others stagnated. He also develops an analytical framework to explore the process of economic change or the lack of it. The most direct and succinct application of his thinking to growth and development is contained in his Gunnar Myrdal Lecture, sponsored by the United Nations Economic Commission for Europe (2003).

In terms of the broader framework that he uses, human societies are viewed as distinct from other species in that they are constantly evolving and, as such, manifest no underlying ergodic structure that social science could be directed at revealing (2005, p. 50). The only social constant is that human action changes the physical and human environment (2005, p. 21). Thus, because institutions need to constantly evolve to adapt to the changing environment, there is no guarantee that erstwhile successful institutions would serve well in the future (2005, pp. 124–125). Institutions are defined as formal rules (constitutions, laws, and regulations), informal rules (norms and conventions, internally held codes of conduct) and enforcement mechanisms (state, society) (2003, p. 2; 2005, p. 3).

Human society is also distinct in manifesting consciousness and "intentionality" in bringing about institutional change to adapt to broader change. Given the various and complex interactions within society, human understanding is limited, so success in framing new institutions is not guaranteed. Failure might also result from the rigidities militating against institutional change ("rules of the game") since the organizations ("players") that embody and benefit from the existing institutional structure have a vested interest in preserving it (2005, pp. 53–59).

North does not view neo-classical economics as an appropriate framework to study development because it is static, assumes perfect information and zero transactions cost ("a friction-less world"), and rejects the idea of intentionality. He concludes that the neo-classical model is better suited to studying resource allocation in high income economies where it evolved. He argues that understanding the world requires a complementary understanding of politics, society and cognitive science, and also of the evolution of cultural heritage (based on religion, myths, superstitions, and prejudices) of particular societies and the associated institutional evolution (2003, p. 1; 2005, p. 18).[2] Institutions facilitate transactions by reducing uncertainty in a world with friction. North acknowledges the importance of preferences, choices, incentives, property rights, and markets that are central to neo-classical economics but their role and importance are theorized differently.[3] Incentives, for example, are considered to be institutions, because they structure human economic interactions and make behavior predictable.

Enforcement is never perfect since the returns on the margin from enhancing enforcement decline relative to the pay-off. However, the degree of imperfection is important and, in this context, politics frame the rules of the market game (2003, p. 4). Politics also determine to whose advantage the rules are framed. The most fundamental rules concern the ownership, use, and alienation of property, as well as the enforcement of contracts (2003, p. 4).

Path dependence can move society towards either prosperity or decline. For example, factors like religion or geography can influence cultural beliefs, which can in turn shape good or bad institutions, leading to either good or bad polities (2003, pp. 5–6; 2005, pp. 50, 58). North clarifies that path dependence is perpetuated by organizations whose survival depends on the survival of existing institutions, so the concept should not be simplistically interpreted as inertia (2005, p. 51).

Culture represents the intergenerational transfer of norms, values, and beliefs. There is a suggestion that religion is endogenous and produces beliefs consistent with the demographic and resource constrains embedded in the geography. For example, the Christian religious framework was suited to the adaptations (institutional and organization changes) congenial to growth. However, the evolution of collectivist rather than the individualist culture that emerged from Muslim religious practice was less suited to impersonal market exchange (2005, pp. 135–136).

The most fundamental transition in human economic interactions is the transition from personal exchange (barter) to impersonal exchange (market).[4] This transition is facilitated by institutions (property rights) and well-functioning organizations that embody these institutions (banks, corporations), as well as enforcement mechanisms (low cost and efficient judicial systems) that boost productivity, induce cooperation, and punish defection. States in poor societies fail to achieve this institutional framework, and hence fail to encourage transactions and growth (pp. 134–135). Conversely, in prosperous societies cultural heritage can shape economic and political institutions that facilitate cooperative behavior and hence reduce transactions cost (2003, p. 8; 2005, pp. 18, 135–136).[5]

Order in society reduces uncertainty and hence facilitates transactions. This can be attained at low cost if there is a shared system of norms and beliefs that are consistent with the rule of law, and which constrain predatory behavior of individuals and organizations. Western societies benefited from a cultural heritage of participatory and stable political institutions conducive to impersonal exchange with the requisite flexibility to adapt to changes and North traces the historical evolution of these institutions (2005, pp. 107–108). Authoritarianism could work, at least for a while, if the rules imposed by the ruler are viewed by the ruled to be in their self-interest. Many poor societies suffer from the lack of order having neither of these polities (participatory or authoritarian) and are additionally handicapped from having to compete with an already developed world (2005, p. 120).

North's reflections on policy are terse. In a nutshell, the prosperity of nations depends on formal rules, informal rules, and enforcement mechanisms. North argues that only the first of the three is responsive to policy and hence policy economists who derive their inspiration from neo-classical economics emphasized "getting prices right" and "fell flat on their faces over and over again."[6]

Like many development scholars [Singer (Chapter 3) or Amsden (Chapter 7)], North emphasizes the importance of learning. He suggests that supporting institutions and complementarities are likely to make an LIC physicist or chemist marginally more productive when based in an HIC, even though the scarcity of these professionals in LICs would lead neo-classical economists to predict the opposite (2003, p. 7).[7] To offset this, he recommended the development of knowledge systems based on the founding of appropriate institutions and organizations—as done in much of East Asia, most recently in China (see Chapter 7).

Basic Human Needs: ILO[8]

The *International Labor Organization* (ILO, 1977) is credited with developing the "Basic Human Needs" approach in the report it prepared for the June 1976 World Employment Conference.[9] The starting point of this approach was challenging the prevailing view that higher growth would automatically lead to higher employment and improved living standards across the board (p. 15). The report also challenged the assumption that because growth required capital formation inequality should be expected to increase before the fruits of prosperity could be diffused. The ILO argued that waiting for generations for the prosperity to trickle down is "unacceptable in human terms and irresponsible in political terms" (p. 4). Instead, it advocated a strategy for restructuring of growth such that the volume and productivity of employment increased to meet the basic human needs of the population at large; all wanting and available for work should find adequately remunerative work (p. 7). Unemployment was viewed as among the major causes of absolute poverty and inequality (p. 15).

Basic Human Needs were defined as the minimum requirements in a particular climatic, social, and cultural context for a family for personal consumption (food, clothing, shelter) and access to essential services (safe drinking water, sanitation, transportation, health, and education). Further, the delivery mechanism for both goods and services should allow for popular participation in decision making. To achieve this, under- and unemployed workers would need to be utilized by a better allocation of capital and the redistribution of productive resources (p. 32). The rural poor would need to be provided with inputs including land, credit, physical infrastructure, and the extension service in agriculture (p. 43).

Land reform would encourage small farmer agriculture and the report cited evidence to demonstrate that output per land unit was inversely associated with farm size (p. 62). The report also cited evidence suggesting that small scale enterprises embodied higher labor productivity, after accounting for factor market distortions that resulted in greater capital intensity of large scale enterprises (p. 148). Non-farm rural activity could be encouraged by supporting food processing and investing in roads and storage facilities. The increase in the productive employment of the poor would increase food security, help the urban consumer and also raise the demand for basic consumer goods and hence change the pattern of production to one suitable for small scale, employment intensive production using appropriate technology (p. 50) [see Schumacher below].

The report recognized that weak tax administration and weak administrative systems limited the effectiveness of the tax/subsidy mechanism for resource mobilization and reallocation. Nonetheless, it recommended progressive taxation and luxury consumption taxes, again with the aim of changing the consumption pattern and productive structure to a more suitable one. Acknowledging the complex political economy of policy implementation and the resistance from vested interests, the report advocated mass organization and participation, with a major role for unions in this process.

According to the report, the recommended change in productive structure would lead to a higher growth trajectory in the medium and long term, which was necessary to accomplish the basic needs strategy. In the short term, however, there could be a loss in output associated with the change in productive structure (p. 67). Here, there is a call for developed country support via a global compact as is the case of the Millennium Development Goals (MDG) (p. vii). The Basic Human Needs approach is conceptually similar to the Human Development approach, and the call to set and monitor and attain targets by 2000 is a pre-curser to the first and revised MDGs. Even the targets such as enhancing life expectancy, reducing infant mortality, and raising literacy are overlapping (p. viii).

Human development: Amartya Sen

The United Nations Development Program (UNDP) launched *The Human Development Report* in 1990 under the leadership of Mahbub ul Haq. Amartya Sen was the advisor to the UNDP to assist in the conceptualization of how development was to be measured using the composite Human Development Index. Choice was the central element in this conceptualization and so the specific indicators in the composite were selected because they were central to enhancing human choice. Per capita GDP was included because it provided the wherewithal for choice, education because it enhanced the quality of choice, and life expectancy because it enabled choice to be exercised over a longer period.

Choice remained central to Sen's conceptualization of development, but it was broadened in *Development as Freedom* (1999). This brought together many of Sen's earlier works to demonstrate that "expansion of freedom is both the primary end and principal means of development" (p. 11). Various rights, opportunities, and entitlements expand freedoms, which have both an intrinsic and instrumental value. Freedom is understood as freedom from deprivation, so development can be thought of as a process of removing "unfreedoms" (p. 37). While the focus is on delivering a similar bundle of goods and services as in the Basic Human Needs approach, the conceptualization is broader and more far reaching.

Freedoms could be classified into five distinct types including political (civil liberties, elections), economic, social opportunities (education, health), transparency guarantees, and protective security (social safety nets) (p. 10). Sen illustrates with evidence and many examples throughout the book how these freedoms are mutually reinforcing in building individual capabilities. Better education and health would improve productivity and raise economic participation and also contribute to public resources for more social facilities. Similarly, political freedom would require delivering to constituencies and so a greater likelihood of the provision of social and economic facilities (p. 10). While the instrumental value of freedoms is important, so is the constitutive value (p. 17).

He argues that on the one hand, based on the empirics, there is no assurance that growth-led processes would deliver freedoms. On the other hand, support-led processes such that those employed in Costa Rica, Sri Lanka, and Kerala, India delivered in this regard. It is not necessary to wait for growth and high per capita GDP to remove deprivations since services are labor intensive. Obviously, the resources growth generates are more effective in removing deprivations if well used (p. 46). Nonetheless, countries that have built a base of capabilities and freedoms with improved education, nutrition, health, and physical infrastructure have also laid the foundation of higher labor productivity and of seizing the opportunities that globalization has to offer. Sen views investment in social and physical infrastructure as the reason for China's superior economic performance relative to India in the globalization context (p. 144).

Sen's preference is for economic growth to be delivered by political freedoms including civil liberties that build pressure for change via voting, criticizing (investigative journalism), public debate and discussion, and protesting (p. 148).[10] For Sen, the premise that human agency is expanded by political liberties is evidenced by the fact that famines have never occurred in a democracy (p. 16). Like other freedoms, political freedoms have instrumental and intrinsic value (p. 152). The political process is value-forming and also provides a path to securing economic freedoms. However, just as in the case of interfacing with economic globalization, opportunities are created but they need to be seized for good outcomes for the poor and society in general.

Sen introduced new terminology to put across his approach to development. Entitlements like endowments and assets build elementary capabilities so people can avoid starvation, undernourishment, premature mortality, and morbidity that emanate from the lack of services such as clean drinking water and sanitation (p. 36). Capabilities are the substantive freedoms that enable individuals to "enjoy the kind of life they have reason to value" and hence they have intrinsic merit. Capabilities refer to "alternative combinations of 'functionings' that are feasible to achieve" such as in participating in the life of a community or in attaining higher life expectancy. The functioning vector identifies the actual achievements based on the choices exercised whereas the capability set is the freedom to achieve (p. 75).

The process of attaining freedoms includes institutions that assure meaningful jobs, public facilities, law and order, social tolerance, and political and civil liberties (p. 4). More important, the process must include agency (ability to act and bring about change) of individuals to participate rather than be mere beneficiaries (pp. 18–19). Markets are an important mechanism for attaining economic growth and access to markets is also important as a basic freedom or liberty to make exchanges (p. 4, Chapter 5).

Sen focuses on increasing capabilities, rather than income, because the instrumental value of income in attaining capability and functionings varies across individuals depending on their age, gender, and ability (p. 89). Thus relative deprivation in income can yield absolute deprivation in capabilities and functionings and real poverty is the lack of capabilities and functionings. Since functionings like nourishment, longevity, health, and literacy are easier to observe and services are less subject to hiding or reselling than income or goods, this approach to reducing poverty is preferable (pp. 131–134). In this regard, he views economists as having focused too narrowly on income poverty (pp. 107–108).

Sen provides philosophical and theoretical support for his approach. He argues that this freedom-based perspective on social justice has greater breath and sensitivity than the utilitarian, libertarian or Rawlsian perspectives (Chapter 3). A theory of justice need only identify "patent injustice" and not necessarily provide an exact distribution, which needs to depend on public discussion and debate (p. 287).

Using similar assumptions required to demonstrate the Arrow-Debreu (Chapter 5, fn. 11) result of the non-improvability of market outcomes, he cites work where he has shown that this result extends to individual freedoms to choose commodity baskets and the capability and funtionings derived from them (pp. 117). The latter result does not require self-interested behavior since the issue at hand is simply the extension of freedoms (p. 118). Since the income earning abilities of the elderly, infirm, and handicapped with the same freedoms would be much lower, the efficiency result based on freedoms is consistent with high inequality and hence the need for intervention from the state and non-state actors to remove deprivations (pp. 119, 287). Individual responsibility can only be expected in the context of ensuring freedoms (p. 284).

Participation: Robert Chambers

While the ILO mentioned participation and Sen emphasized it even more, both as a means of attaining development and as a marker for measuring development, it is probably Chambers who has done more than any other scholar or practitioner to popularize the concept of participation, particularly in the context of rural development. Chambers finds all poverty outrageous but focuses on rural poverty since it is less visible (1983, p. 3). He writes with intense passion and commitment about eliminating poverty.

Chambers' official profile states he has a background in biology, history, and public administration and he takes a dim view of economists (1997, pp. 49–53).[11] Nonetheless, by popularizing qualitative research methods, he has done development economics and the social sciences a service. Participation has been put forward as a tool for learning about development. It is also put forward as a mechanism for attaining development by encouraging collective action by the poor, mobilized, or encouraged to draw on their own knowledge.

In a review article (1994), Chambers explains the origins of its use in development research to five roots including activist participatory research, agro-ecosystem analysis, applied anthropology, field research in farming systems, and rapid rural appraisal. The activist participatory research inspired by Paulo Freire, suggesting that the "poor should be enabled to conduct their own analysis of their own reality," was seminal in how these roots merged into the method of participatory appraisal (pp. 954–955).

Rapid rural appraisal (RRA) (late 1970s, 1980s) was the most immediate precursor of the evolving participatory rural appraisal (late 1980s onward). RRA was a qualitative research method that emerged to address the numerous shortcomings of conventional survey research and also of the various biases inherent in gleaning quick rural knowledge.[12] RRA gradually acquired respect-ability in academia as a cost effective method that could actually be optimal (p. 956). RRA started to engage in participatory methods and for these to work the outsiders needed both the patience to listen, and the humility to acknow-ledge that they could learn from the poor, who possessed authentic knowledge (p. 963).

Yet RRA had its own shortcomings; the most important criticism was that RRA was eliciting or extractive to serve an academic agenda. Participatory Rural Appraisal (PRA), in its ideal form, addressed these shortcomings and, instead of using local people's knowledge for scholarly attainment, aimed to facilitate or catalyze the locals' analytical abilities for a genuinely bottom-up approach to development rather than the other conventional top-down approaches. The objective is not to have local people learn from outsiders, but to empower locals to perform their own analysis and engage in sustainable collective action that leads to institutional change (p. 958).

In *Rural Development: Putting the Last First* (1983) and *Whose Reality Counts: Putting the Last First* (1997) Chambers expands on the themes above and, based on experience acquired from the field, documents best practice. He makes a case for a hybrid "inventive and eclectic" cost effective case study ("fairly quick and fairly clean") that draws on the strengths of other methods but avoids the "quick and dirty" of development tourism, the "long and dirty" of the questionnaire survey, or the prolonged immersion of the social anthropologists (1983, pp. 71, 199–200).[13]

There is now a plethora of well-documented tools used in qualitative research, including: semi-structured interviews, working with key informants and focus groups, engaging in transect walks, mapping, and modeling using local mater-ials, drawing on oral histories, matrix scoring and ranking, time lines, livelihood and time use analysis and finally presentation and analysis.[14] Participation has become a central aspect of other approaches to development including those that preceded this section and the two that follow in this chapter.

Gender and development[15]

As in the rest of the book, this section highlights key authors and themes. While exploring the broader debate, it does not explore the particular debates in the field, in this case the one that took the field from "women in development" to "women and development" and on to "gender in development" and currently "gender and development" or the associated criticisms.[16] I selected Esther Boserup (1910–1999) because her contribution is widely acknowledged to be seminal, Gita Sen and Caren Grown because they emphasize the importance of the larger macro and structural context, and Bina Agarwal because she emphasizes the importance of the micro or household level context as a foundation for macro policy responses.[17]

In *Woman's Role in Economic Development* (1986), Esther Boserup addressed what she saw as the lack of attention to "the problems of women" in the ever growing economic development literature. Her focus was on the sex-pattern of productive work emerging from the modernization of agriculture and rural-urban migration. In this process, she saw work becoming more hierarchical. Women were systematically denied education and perceived as inferior; as a consequence they were confined to unskilled, routine, and low productivity work utilizing primitive equipment. Agricultural modernization, which might have militated to their advantage by reducing the premium on physical strength, actually bypassed women because men monopolized the more efficient equipment operated with animal or mechanical power. Thus women continued with traditional activities and methods. Boserup viewed the male attitudes of European colonizers as reinforcing male hierarchy in work (p. 53). The extension service was exclusively for males, cash crops remained a male preserve, and land reform privileged males (p. 58).

Even in home industries, male skills were privileged. For example, in the batik home industry in Jogjakarta, Indonesia, printing was considered "skilled" labor and commanded a higher wage, whereas the women's work of waxing and scraping were delineated as "trained" rather than skilled activities, which paid less despite being equally difficult (p. 108). Women were again sidelined when modern forms of industry and trade replaced traditional market trade. Men secured the clerical jobs and, after independence, the administrative and managerial jobs, while women were confined to the unskilled and subservient positions (Chapters 5 and 6).

Boserup challenged the prevailing view that women should take the back seat in employment in industry to accommodate men as the primary breadwinners. She argued that women competing for all jobs would not only enhance society's productive potential but would also reduce the subjective probabilities of rural migrants in their assessment of urban job prospects.[18] This would thus reduce migration and simultaneously enhance food production, particularly in conjunction with improved agriculture. In addition, it would stimulate economic growth, reduce urban infrastructure needs, and enhance tax revenue (Chapter 11).

In *Development, Crises, and Alternative Visions*, Gita Sen and Caren Grown (1987) challenge the view that integrating women into the development process by ensuring better education, jobs, credit, assets, and income is enough (p. 15). They viewed the struggle as a broader one of challenging structures that resulted in national, racial, class, ethnic, caste, as well as gender oppression. Thus simply seeking equality for women in a broader unequal context is unlikely to be enough. For example, seeking equality with men subject to low wages and poor working conditions is not a worthy goal for them (p. 25). They viewed oppressive structures as often having emerged from colonial domination but also as having been perpetuated and reinforced in a post-colonial world due to the enmeshed interests of powerful international and national elites (p. 26).

Sen and Grown propose that the appropriate mechanism for changing these structures is social mobilization that builds pressure for land reform, addresses basic needs "with people-centered approaches," and evens out inequalities in income and wealth. This would unleash the productive potential of agriculture and shared prosperity would create a domestic market. In addition, they recommend improving the productive capacity and working conditions in the informal sector, where women are predominant. Women, as the collectors of food, fuel, and water, and also as food workers and processors, need also to be recognized as central to resolving the triple crises of food, water, and fuel, which plague poor countries (p. 57).

Given this central role as providers, structural adjustment programs have the greatest impact on women as the state cuts back on social services and subsidies. Women subsequently have to make do with less and their work burden rises (p. 63). Instead of this austerity, Sen and Grown suggest that women need to be accorded equal status during and after productivity enhancing land reforms (p. 84) and provided access to credit, technology, and markets to address the triple crises (p. 51).

Bina Agarwal (1988, pp. 86–88) focused on household gender disparities in the broader social and economic context, looking particularly at how development strategies and consequent ecological degradation impacted poor rural women. Agarwal cited available evidence from India to demonstrate that poor rural women often worked longer than men and that, despite getting paid less for the same agricultural tasks, women's gross contribution, including "invisible" non-market work that men did not acknowledge, to their households was greater. Even so, women's and girls' access to crucial needs like food and health, based on intra-household distribution, was less than that of men's and boys', accounting for systematic gender differentials in malnutrition, morbidity, and mortality. Such differentials intensified in lean periods (p. 89). Labor force participation rates and marriage costs (dowry or bride price) were among the factors that accounted for such differences and these in turn were shaped by factors such as history, culture, and geography (pp. 92–95).[19]

Agarwal points out that the ecological degradation of the commons and deforestation add to women's burden of gathering food, water, and fuel (1988, p. 86). Deforestation reduces ground water recharge and also reduces the availability of the forest products that poor women traditionally harvested. Agarwal further contrasts the harvesting of twigs and dead branches by the rural poor with the clearcutting of forests to meet urban needs. The clearing of old forests for commercial planting, privatization, and illegal encroachment of commons all displaced traditional rights (p. 111). The High Yielding Variety water-intensive crops that were part of the "Green Revolution" package also lowered the water table adding to the burden of water collection for women (pp. 105–108). This development initiative resulted in women's exposure to toxic chemicals when working in the fields.

In *A Field of One's Own* (1994), Agarwal makes a powerful multi-pronged and carefully argued case for extending both land ownership and control (since the latter does not follow automatically from the former) to women (pp. 27–45).[20] The most compelling elements in this case include the need for social security if women are deserted, divorced or widowed. Land provides more assurance of shelter and livelihood than any other support mechanism. She pointed out that for the land distribution to work, even more so the case than for land reform in general, technical (access to extension service), and institutional support (access to input and product markets) would need to be provided.

She accepted Amartya Sen's (1990) cooperative-conflict model of intra-household decision making as superior to the implicit neo-classical or even Marxist view of a benign male household head acting in the household interest (1992, p. 183). Having argued that women's bargaining power essentially depends on their fall-back position (i.e. their ability to cope without the male spouse or male household head), Agarwal noted that women's bargaining power within the household is strengthened by ownership and control of assets (particularly land), access to employment or other income earning opportunities, communal resources, and kin and other support networks (p. 185).

What follows from Agarwal's analysis of intra-household bargaining is that rather than gender-blind public support for poverty alleviation, which in effect means support for male household heads, policy concerned with women as the most vulnerable would need to be more focused on strengthening women's fall-back position. This could include enforcement of legal property rights, expansion of income-earning opportunities, and strengthening of communal control over village commons and forests (p. 203).[21] Since the state could be part of the problem, such as with regards to skewed privatization of commons and deforestation, she suggests that social mobilization or group organization is necessary in order to pressure the state to help strengthen the bargaining position of women (p. 204).

Sustainable development

The ecologically sensitive writings of Ernst Friedrich Schumacher (1911–1977) far preceded the invention of the term "sustainable development," a broad term that now incorporates economic and social development and ecological sustainability. Schumacher was among the first development economists to give voice to the growing ecological concerns being expressed in the early 1970s, and he is notable for his concern with holistic development. He popularized the view that the economic system was on a collision course with nature and the ecological system. This collision was even more likely due to the aspirations of poor countries to pursue the path of the rich ones.

His classic book *Small is Beautiful* (1974) brought together several of his writings. According to Schumacher, neither mainstream economists nor Marxists had properly acknowledged and accounted for the use of natural capital in production and this created an incentive for overuse of natural resources. He suggested that fossil fuels should be treated as natural capital rather than an income flow. If the use of natural capital was thus appropriately accounted for, this would rightly create an incentive to conserve fossil fuels, rather than to maximize their use in the process of maximizing production (p. 12). He recommended that the income drawn from the use of natural capital should be placed in a fund to develop alternatives to fossil fuels (as Norway subsequently did). For example, the fund could finance the development of clean energy that is environmentally benign.

He also worried that in the quest to maximize GDP, scientists had created compound substances that nature had no defense against such as chemical fertilizers and insecticides that were part of the "Green Revolution" package. Thus, he advocated an eco-friendly organic agriculture along with incentives to change the consumption pattern in rich countries (p. 14).

He analyzed the associated twin problem of unemployment and rural-urban migration as the critical problem in LICs. This pattern resulted from a mutual poisoning: urban bias and industry ruined rural areas by devastating agriculture sector and crafts, while rural-urban migration resulted in sprawl, blight, and instability in cities (p. 136).

Aid was mostly misplaced because it failed to recognize that the base of development was education, organization, and discipline. Functioning factories and other institutions in HICs are built on these foundations, which evolve slowly. Aid would do best in building this base in LICs and the best place to start would be gleaning the knowledge that would contribute to aid effectiveness (pp. 160–171).

Schumacher's other contribution to development economics was in devising more appropriate employment friendly "intermediate technology". Such technology, he argued, fitted between primitive and advanced capital intensive modern technology to address the rural and urban informal sector unemployment problem. Schumacher turned the economic problem on its head. Instead of maximizing production and consumption (profits and utility), he proposed organizing the economy around maximizing meaningful jobs. For LICs, this would mean using appropriate technology that was inexpensive, easily accessible, small scale, and compatible with the human need for creativity (p. 27).[22] The "workplaces" created with such technology would conserve on capital, foreign exchange (use local materials), skills, finance and marketing, organization, supervision, and repair and maintenance (pp. 146–151). Employment is the pre-condition of everything else in a market economy and so a market would be assured. Those willing to develop intermediate technology would find applications in water and power, crop-storage, food processing, health, and transport. Thus, a new agro-industrial culture could be created.[23]

Schumacher viewed the practice of mainstream economists as wrong-headed; they in turn saw him as a pariah. Yet, Schumacher was part of the inspiration for the environmental movement and gained a loyal following. These ideas are evident in a landmark study *Our Common Future* (also called the Brundtland Report, after lead author Gro Harkem Brundtland), written on behalf of the UN World Commission on Environment and Development. This report, more than any other document, created a momentum for the sustainable development approach. In fact, one of its fundamental contributions was proposing a definition of the concept.

Sustainable development enjoins humanity "to ensure that it meets the needs of the present without compromising the ability of future generations to meet its own needs" (p. 8). This brief definition, while it cannot be all inclusive, suggested two key concepts: First, meeting essential needs, particularly of the world's poor; second, efforts to meet current needs must be limited to the extent that they affect the environment's ability to meet future needs. The concept of inter-generational equity is explicit and the Bundtland Report states that this concern logically extends to intra-generational equity, so that concern for the poor was central to the definition of sustainable development. Similarly, the concern for the environment extends to a concern for all species (p. 42). The bulk of the report documents the degradation of air, water, and other natural elements and presents suggestions for urgent redress.

Summary, reflection and conclusions

This chapter reviews the work of scholars who do not fit neatly into any mold, but who are mostly focused on issues concerning social justice. While the latter is not a major concern for North, he challenged orthodox thinkers by rejecting neo-classical economics as a useful framework for understanding development. North argues that institutions defined as formal or informal rules and enforcement mechanisms are central to understanding the prosperity of nations or the lack thereof. Societies that have evolved the institutional framework to facilitate the key transformation from personal exchanges to impersonal (market) exchanges keep transactions costs low and expand the market size and are therefore more likely to prosper. While the state is expected to play a critical role in the framing and enforcement of formal rules (such as those pertaining to property rights), the cultural heritage of societies can make the informal rules more or less conducive to cooperative behavior that facilitate exchange. There is a pessimistic note to this theory of development and underdevelopment, since it suggests that poor governance and constraining norms may be part of the cultural heritage and path dependency can project failure into the future.

Although North places choice, incentives, property rights and markets center stage, his theory represents a challenge to the universalism of neo-classical economics as suggested by the writings of Peter T. Bauer and Deepak Lal reviewed in the next chapter. North's emphasis on historical and cultural evolution, gradual institutional change, and path dependency may not be suited to explaining the discrete changes or jumps that have contributed to the history of economic development over the last century, as documented in Chapter 7. Indeed, this history suggests that societies can learn from others and that discrete changes are indeed possible in the form of rapid catch-up growth.

North makes a very effective critique of structural adjustment programs, arguing that their exclusive focus on formal rules dooms them to fail. Yet he makes the ironic observation that LICs need to shift from a society regulated by traditional cultural norms, respect for status and rank, a coercive polity, mutual control, and enforced codes of generosity, into an open society with free entry and exit, democratic governance, and competence criteria (2005, p. 100). This is almost like saying LIC should develop to develop. Indeed, the changes he suggests are likely to be endogenous to the development process rather than prerequisites. Furthermore, North's view of gradual change and path dependency suggests that these norms could not be adopted at will, even if they were preconditions for development.

Institutional change comes into play in the rest of the chapter insofar as it is seen as a means of delivering basic human needs, a connecting theme of the rest of the chapter. Among the various approaches reviewed, other common themes include gender equality, employment, rural to urban migration, asset distribution and land reform, ecology, participation, and international aid.

In the ILO version of the Basic Human Needs approach, the central concept is altering the productive structure to one that would utilize the productive potential of unemployed and underemployed workers, the bulk of whom reside in rural areas. Starting with land reform, infrastructure, input (including credit), and extension support, a more efficient and labor intensive agriculture could be established with small holders as the primary actors and beneficiaries. This agricultural reform would produce a consumption pattern more geared to small scale, labor intensive production. Such production would also be reinforced by removing factor price distortions that privilege capital intensity in large scale enterprises.

The Basic Human Needs approach shared with the mainstream approach a concern with promoting a high-growth path (p. 32) and removing factor price distortions (p. 51), but it differed in its focus (employment) and goals (meeting basic human needs). It also shared with the mainstream approach a concern with free trade based on factor endowments, although it anticipated more inter-LIC trade since these countries would be closer to each other's productive trajectories. It also advocated the concept of dynamic comparative advantage by anticipating that as productive structures evolved and changed, comparative advantage would change (p. 105).

The Basic Human Needs approach was extended and transformed by Amartya Sen in his capacity as an advisor to the United Nations Development Program's human development approach, which centered on development as enhancing choice. Sen extended this approach to development as enhancing freedoms.

Freedoms represent both the principal means and primary ends of development. Development as a process requires extending entitlements (assets, facilities, services) to build capabilities that result in functionings such as higher literacy and life expectancy. Human agency is central to the development process, and derives in part from political and civil liberties, open debate, and even protest if necessary, all of which serve to demonstrate need, frame objectives, and build pressure for delivery. Historically, agency is seized or conceded due to pressure from below, so the democratic process provides an important avenue for the success of Sen's approach. Sen provides philosophical and theoretical support for his approach.

Robert Chambers has elaborated on participation as the mechanism central to Sen's approach. Development, for Chambers, is the institutional change and empowerment that results from the poor taking action based on their knowledge and analysis to improve their condition. Thus, participation is viewed as a mechanism for the poor to generate knowledge and social analysis for their own use. Chambers views conventional survey research as seriously flawed, presumptuous, condescending, and extractive. The poor possess authentic social knowledge and outsiders can be facilitators, catalysts and even learners, provided that they themselves possess the requisite humility. The state could facilitate this process. While this may seem far-fetched, Chambers acknowledges this to be an ideal.

Esther Boserup explored the gender implications of the changing pattern of work involved in the process of economic development arguing that women became worse off in all sectors. In agriculture, men appropriated technological change that eased the work burden while women continued with traditional agriculture. In the modern sector, men who got privileged access to education also got access to the higher level jobs while women were confined to the low skilled, low paying jobs.

Sen and Gower broaden this critique and explore gender oppression in the context of post-colonial, class, racial, ethnic, and caste oppression. They argue that none of these structures can be addressed without changing the social systems creating the oppression. The solution they propose is to implement land reforms that privilege women and directly address gender-related and other inequalities to release agriculture's productive potential and create an internal market for industrialization. Since women manage the production, processing and collection of food, in addition to fuel and water collection, addressing their needs for credit, technology and market access will address the triple crisis of food, water, and fuel poor countries confront. They recommended far-reaching social mobilization among women's organizations, starting from the grassroots level, to build pressure for structural change.

Agarwal explored gender oppression in the intra-household context in which females have less access to food and health care, resulting in a higher female incidence of malnutrition, morbidity, and mortality. Development initiatives such as the green revolution worsened women's position: exposure to chemicals damaged their health, while forest clearing added to their burden of providing for food, fodder, and fuel for the family. Meanwhile, contrary to conventional views on the poverty-environment nexus, women's harvesting did not damage the forests, as did the extensive deforestation undertaken for development initiatives or to meet urban fuel needs. Given this context, Agarwal makes a powerful case on economic and social grounds for extending land ownership and control to women. One part of this case is strengthening women's weak fall-back position in intra-household bargaining. She argues that public policy interventions should strengthen this fall-back position by enforcing entitlements to property, providing income earning opportunities and conserving and ensuring access to common property resources and forests. Since state policy can often be the problem in the latter context, civil society social mobilization can build the requisite pressure for state delivery and right action.

Schumacher could be viewed as among the initiators of the sustainable development approach. He analyzed the problem of ecological disaster as one resulting from overconsumption in the West, where natural capital was viewed as a revenue stream rather than as asset depletion. As a development economist, Schumacher argued that instead of maximizing utility and profits, livelihoods should be maximized using benign intermediate technology that could be locally manufactured, maintained, and improved, and would use local materials. Maximizing livelihoods would address the problems of rural urban migration, unemployment, and urban blight. Schumacher's concerns were taken forward by *Our Common Future*, which was written on behalf of the UN World Commission on Environment and Development, and pushed forward the sustainable development agenda.

Notes

1 North (2001, p. 491) wrote a one page explanation of the theory of change needed which he started by stating "The problems in development economics are straight forward." This section is his elaboration on this theory of change.
2 Development economists in general and those who have read earlier chapters of this volume will recognize that these points have been made by classical and later scholars. However, the insightful way in which North presents these ideas and where he takes them is certainly fresh.
3 North argues that cognitive science assumes importance for choice made under conditions of imperfect information. Also refer to (1990, chapter 3) for a discussion of behavioral assumptions and individual behavior. My focus here, as in the rest of the book, is mainly on macro development economics theory.
4 He refers to overlapping innovations that reduce transactions cost by raising capital mobility, reducing information costs and diffusing risk (1990, pp. 125–130).
5 North's (2005) chapter 10 on the historical evolution of market friendly institutions in the West in particular and the rise of the Western world in general should be compulsory reading for all students of development economics from lower and middle income countries.
6 North is likely to have been influential in the formulation of the second generation of structural adjustment reforms instituted by the Breton Woods organizations emphasizing "good governance" (see Chapter 6).
7 In fact, if one took into account social externalities generated by a physicist or chemist when based in an LIC, this might offset the importance of complementarities. Refer to Khan (2012) for an elaboration on this point.

8 Refer to Hunt (1989) for a review of the basic needs approach. She distinguishes between a reformist approach favored by international financial institutions such as the World Bank that focused on social sector delivery and a more radical approach that included asset (land, credit) distribution and subsequent changing of the structure of consumption and production. For key contributors refer to Streeten (1981) and Stewart (1985).

9 The report drew on Dag Hammarskjöld Foundation (1975).

10 Refer to Sen (2001) for a brief essay in the author's own words advocating the freedom-centered view of development. In this essay Sen cites cross-country studies suggesting that political freedoms are also consistent with economic growth apart from providing protective powers by "giving voice to the deprived and vulnerable" (p. 507). While the latter argument is difficult to contest, the nature of the association between democracy and economic growth has been contested. Refer to Rivera-Batiz and Rivera-Batiz (2002) for a review of the cross-country evidence.

11 Chambers' comparison of economists to dogs marking territory may have offended dog lovers (1997, p. 53).

12 For a critique of the expensive, inaccurate, and ineffective outcomes from the questionnaire survey method, refer to Chambers (1983, pp. 45–58) and for biases inherent in what he dismisses as "quick and dirty development tourism," refer to (1983, pp. 13–23, 199).

13 Social anthropologists [see, for example, (Mosse, 2001)] were not impressed with this attempt to incorporate their painstaking method of learning into a "quick and dirty" PRA method, as subject to abuse as the ones Chambers criticized.

14 Chambers (1997, chapters 6 and 7) elaborates on these tools and concedes that since much participatory analysis and work has been done in urban areas, it would make sense to refer to the method as Participatory Learning and Action (PLA). However, he notes that the term PRA has acquired a life of its own (1997, xvii).

15 For a comprehensive collection of major contributions in the gender and development field, refer to eds. Banería and Bisnath (2001).

16 Those writing on human development in a broader context also write about gender and development and vice versa with scholars aware of the mutual interactions in the approaches. See for example Amartya Sen's (1999, chapter 8) contributions on women's agency or Gita Sen and Caren Grown's (1987) recognition of the mutuality of oppression and for common solutions based on structural change.

17 Diane Elson, among many others, is another key writer in this field but since much of her work is in the context of structural adjustment I have referred to this work in Chapter 7. Thanks are due to Gunseli Bérik and Avanti Mukerjee for suggestions.

18 Refer to Chapter 2, en. 22.

19 Since males in many poor households counted as below the headcount poverty line had nutrition levels above the cut-off and vice versa for females in households counted as above the poverty line, she suggested that the official poverty statistics were likely to understate poverty (p. 85).

20 A similar distinction between ownership and control has been made in the context of microcredit loans ostensibly given to females but used by male household members (Parmar, 2003).

21 Here Agarwal distinguishes between entitlements and enforcement. While both are needed, the lack of enforcement of existing entitlements like female land rights can be the problem (p. 203).

22 This is a radical proposal and has far-reaching implications for the relative role of the market and state.

23 Schumacher inspired many with his approach to poverty alleviation and the Intermediate Technology Development Group he co-founded is still active, among other groups, in trying to realize a mission statement derived from his work. For a critique of intermediate technology refer to Emmanuel (chapter 3).

References

Agarwal, B. 1994. *A Field of One's Own. Cambridge*: Cambridge University Press.

Agarwal, B. 1992. "Gender Relations and Food Security: Coping with Seasonality, Drought, and Famine in South Asia." In: L. Bénería and S. Feldman, eds., *Unequal Burden: Economic Crisis, Persistent Poverty, and Women's Work*. Boulder: Westview Press.

Agarwal, B. 1988. "Neither Sustenance nor Sustainability: Agricultural Strategies, Ecological Degradation and Indian Women in Poverty." In: B. Agarwal, ed., *Structures of Patriarchy: The State, The Community and the Household*. London: Zed Books.

Banería, L. and Bisnath, S., eds., 2001. *Gender and Development: Theoretical, Empirical and Practical Approaches*. Northampton, Massachusetts: Edward Elgar.

Boserup, E. 1986. *Women's Role in Economic Development*. Aldershot, Hants: Gower.

Chambers, R. 1997. *Whose Reality Counts: Putting the Last First*. 2nd edition. London: Intermediate Technology Publications.

Chambers, R. 1994. "The Origins and Practice of Participatory Rural Appraisal." *World Development*, 22 (7), 953–969.

Chambers, R. 1983. *Rural Development: Putting the Last First*. Essex: Longman Scientific and Technical.

Dag Hammarskjöld Foundation Report on Development and International Cooperation. 1975. *What Now: Another Development* prepared on the occasion of the Seventh Special Session of the United Nations General Assembly, New York, 1–12 September 1975, Uppsala, Sweden.

Hunt, D. 1989. *Economic Theories of Development: An Analysis of Competing Paradigms*. Savage, Maryland: Barnes & Noble Books.

ILO (International Labor Organization). 1977. *Employment, Growth and Basic Needs: A One World Problem*. New York: Praeger.

Khan, S. R. 2012. "Highly Educated Emigration from Low Income Countries: Turning pain to gain." In: K. Khory, ed., *Global Migration: Challenges in the Twenty-First Century*. New York: Palgrave Macmillan.

Mosse, D. 2001. "People's knowledge, participation, and patronage: Operations and representations in rural development." In: B. Cooke and U. Kothari, eds., *Participation: The New Tyranny*. London: Zed Press.

North, D. C. 2005. *Understanding the Process of Economic Change*. Princeton: Princeton University Press.

North, D. C. 2003. "The Role of Institutions in Economic Development." Gunnar Myrdal Lecture. Occasional Paper No. 1. New York and Geneva: Economic Commission for Europe. United Nations.

North, D. C. 2001. "Needed: A Theory of Change." In: Gerald M. Meier and Joseph E. Stiglitz, eds., *Frontiers of Development Economics: The Future in Perspective*. Oxford: World Bank and Oxford University Press.

North, D. C. 1990. *Institutions, Institutional Change and Performance*. Cambridge: Cambridge University Press.

Parmar, A. 2003. "Micro-Credit, Empowerment, and Agency: Re-evaluating the Discourse." *Canadian Journal of Development Studies*, 24 (3), 461–476.

Rivera-Batiz, F. L. and Rivera-Batiz, L. A. 2002. "Democracy, Participation and Development," *Review of Development Economics*, 6 (2), 135–150.

Schumacher, E. F. 1974. *Small is Beautiful: A Study of Economics as if People Mattered*. London: ABACUS.

Sen, G. and Grown, C. 1987. *Development, Crises, and Alternative Visions*. New York: Monthly Review Press.

Sen, A. K. 2001. "What is Development About?" In: G. M. Meier and J. E. Stiglitz, eds., *Frontiers of Development Economics: The Future in Perspective*. Oxford: World Bank and Oxford University Press.

Sen, A. K. 1999. *Development as Freedom*. New York: Anchor Books.

Sen, A. K. 1990. "Gender and Co-Operative Conflicts." In: I. Tinker, eds., *Persistent Inequalities: Women and World Development*. New York: Oxford University Press.

Streeten, P. 1981. *First Things First: Meeting Basic Needs in Developing Countries*. Oxford: Oxford University Press.

Stewart, F. 1985. *Planning to Meet Basic Needs*. London: Macmillan.

UNWCD (World Commission on Environment and Development). 1987. *Our Common Future*. Oxford: Oxford University Press.

Part III

The neo-classical counter-challenge

6 Neo-liberalism and the Washington Consensus

Introduction

The liberal counter-challenge to developmentalism emerged almost concurrently with developmentalist thinking. Early on, Bauer and Yamey (1957) took issue with the developmentalists, most prominently on questioning the implied developmentalist role of government. In challenging developmentalist assumptions, they introduced notions of rent seeking, capture, and government failure into the development debate. However, faith in the government's ability to initiate development remained strong throughout the 1950s, the heady early days of developmentalism. Thus, it took a while for what came to be called "neo-liberalism" to become ascendant.

One could think of neo-liberalism as the manifestation of liberal economic philosophy in specific policy prescriptions associated with the World Bank and the IMF. Apart from the conceptual work of liberal writers like Bauer (1972, 1984) and Lal (1983), major empirical research projects sponsored by the Organization for Economic Cooperation and Development (OECD) and the National Bureau of Economic Research (NBER) accumulated evidence to challenge the prescribed developmentalist role of government. However, it was not until the political climate shifted that neo-liberalism took hold.[1]

The political climate shifted in the early 1980s. At that time, the ascendancy of conservative politicians in the US, UK, and Germany set the stage for the neo-liberal counter revolution to developmentalist thinking. Furthermore, the debt crisis of the early 1980s caused many countries to turn to the World Bank and IMF for support and this enabled the latter to implement a neo-liberal economic program based on structural adjustment as an operational program.

While the agency of private capital and governments were important in shaping and implementing a neo-liberal agenda, a greater emphasis is usually placed on the role of the World Bank and IMF in advancing this process. There are several reasons for the emphasis on these institutions. First, their very well-staffed and richly endowed research departments have been central in continuing to build the intellectual case for neo-liberalism; directly via in-house research and indirectly via contract research. Second, other western aid agencies have actively implemented the proscribed foreign investment- and market-friendly agenda via engineered policy coherence (Grabel, 2010). Third, while there may appear to have been a greater acceptance and a voluntary turn to neo-liberal policies in several countries, Grabel shows that neo-liberal influence can be direct via conditional loans or indirect via leadership capture. Fourth, private capital has in general followed the lead of these institutions in judging whether or not the countries are capital friendly. Being subject to the discipline of a structural adjustment program has been perceived as a positive signal in this regard.

Key thinkers

Péter Tamás Bauer (1915–2002)[2]

Bauer's time came in the 1980s and he was made a baron by conservative Prime Minister Margaret Thatcher. Bauer and Yamey's (1957) definition of development at first sight is remarkably like the definition of development in the UNDP's Human Development Reports launched in 1990 as extending the "range of choices" for humans. Bauer and Yamey also indicate a preference for a society in which policy is directed towards widening "the range of effective choice" for members of a society (p. 149). This is both the policy objective and the criterion by which to ascertain if development had been attained. But while the UNDP's reference is to humans and the objective of policy to attain equality of opportunity as defined by Myrdal (see Chapter 4), Bauer and Yamey intend their definition to apply to individuals as producers and consumers (p. 150) and hence their vision is liberal in the classical sense. While they are not opposed to policy, the advocacy is for policy to facilitate the market by enhancing knowledge available to economic actors.[3]

This concern with individual liberty has Austrian origins and following from this school of thought Bauer and Yamey's unique contribution to development economics pertained to the limited role of government. They introduced into development economics the notion of government failure and of efficacy of decentralized coordination by the market, citing Hayek to make this point (p. 155). Government failure thus represents the theory of underdevelopment and the theory of development is the market based effective deployment of resources, based on the mechanisms of fuller knowledge mobilization and full play given to incentives (p. 154).[4] Private enterprise is also deemed as more than just production by state owned enterprises since those who fail to meet the test of market competitiveness suffer losses while the tax payers foot the bill for mistakes made by state owned enterprises (p. 155).[5]

Bauer and Yamey also deconstructed the concept of government, questioning the motives of functionaries, as did later public choice theorists. They pointed out that economic bureaucrats and other policy makers would not necessarily act in the public interest, and were free to pursue personal agendas of maximizing power (empire building), prestige, position, and economic interests. (p. 156). In fact, given that most of the powerful decision makers are based in urban areas, they are likely to bias the process of resource allocation to enrich these areas, thereby disadvantaging the rural areas where the bulk of the population resides (p. 155).[6]

Bauer and Yemey noted that market competition acts as countervailing power to check inefficient firms, but lamented that there are no such checks to discipline public officials whose abuse of office creates waste and inefficiency. Since this is more likely to be the case in underdeveloped countries, a stronger case for limiting the economic role of government there follows (p. 157). In any case, the state would never have the same success as investment bankers and financial firms in selecting appropriate activities, and would therefore risk misallocating resources and creating corruption in the process (p. 202).[7]

They were unconvinced of the necessity for state intervention because they were not persuaded of the existence of market failures such as limited horizons, spillover effects, discontinuities, or imperfect capital markets.[8] They cited evidence from Malaya and Sumatra indicating that producers were prepared to plant rubber trees given the right incentives even though the gestation period was long (p. 158) and asserted that if profitable opportunities are available, then funds should be available (p. 192). Positive externalities are yielded by knowledge and providing information and advice as a public good, and that is what the state should focus on, such as in the case of agricultural extension (pp. 159, 217–219).[9]

They further challenged the developmentalists' special focus on manufacturing as economically unwarranted, claiming that industrialization was merely a political objective since there was nothing special about it and agriculture was better suited to absorb surplus labor anyway (pp. 193, 237). They suggest that they are many paths to growth and the one adopted must be the sum of dispersed decision making such that individual preferences of consumers and producers are given full play.[10]

In this vision of decentralized development, Bauer (1984, p. 12) draws on his West African experience to celebrate the positive economic role played by traders. Far from being exploitative middlemen, he argued, these individuals stimulate economic activity, including farming, by providing inputs and marketing cash crops, as well as providing inducement goods.[11] They improve transportation, engage in manufacturing, generate entrepreneurial activity, provide tax revenue to the state, and acquaint others with the working of an exchange economy and the attitudes appropriate to associated transactions.[12] Bauer deplored that the state displaced them with inefficient monopsonistic marketing boards that underpaid farmers (p. 14).

In his early writings, Bauer was not opposed to aid. He conceded that foreign capital, including grants, could play a complementary role in development, while agreeing with most developmentalists that domestic saving must play the primary role. However, he argued that aid should only be made available "to countries which agree to follow the right economic policies," and might thus have been one of the first scholars to advocate conditional aid. Appropriate policy for him was promoting the market order (1957, p. 142). In his subsequent writings, however—notably *Dissent on Development* (1972) and *Reality and*

Rhetoric (1984)—he was more hostile to aid, viewing it on balance as doing more harm than good.

In *Dissent on Development* (1972, p. 99), as in other works, Bauer declared the prime determinants of development to be "economic aptitudes, social institutions, and political arrangements." If these conditions are in place, aid is redundant. If they are not in place, aid cannot create them—it merely addresses the symptoms created by the absence of these fundamental conditions. He pointed out that HICs had all managed to develop without aid, and used this as further evidence to show that aid was not necessary (p. 97).[13]

In *Reality and Rhetoric* Bauer's opposition was premised on aid not going to those in whose name it was justified, but instead to support unsavory, retrogressive, and destructive regimes that used it to politicize economic life (p. 46). He argued that the individuals who actually benefited from the aid were more prosperous that the average western taxpayer, and that much of the aid was frittered away in prestige projects which contributed negative value added. Multi-lateral aid was worse since it was less effective and there was even less accountability to tax payers. Unfortunately, it was defended and promoted by aid bureaucracies that, like other bureaucracies, were driven by empire building motives and sought to expand the volume and scope of their activities (p. 65). Bauer saw evidence of aid ineffectiveness in the growing indebtedness of many LICs, and suggested that if there really were a worthy project that could pay back the principle and interest, it would find the funding (p. 48).

Empirical support countering developmentalism

While Bauer was a contemporary of the developmentalists, his ideas did not garner attention until they were supported by empirical findings. Little, Scitovsky, and Scott (1970) were commissioned by the OECD to explore the outcome of the strategy adopted by the key countries based on developmentalist prescriptions. The project was conceived in 1965 and it drew on six volumes representing seven country studies including Argentina (based on existing material), Brazil, India, Mexico, Pakistan, the Philippines, and Taiwan.

Little, Skitovsky, and Scott's key finding was that industrialization had been overencouraged relative to agriculture, that exports had been discouraged, and that inequality had been exacerbated. They contended that there was not enough empirical evidence on positive external economies to justify a special role for industry and in any case the negative environmental externalities were being ignored (pp. 124–125).[14] Overall they concluded that Import Substitution Industrialization (ISI) was harmful since high-cost, inefficient, often public enterprises were being supported with an overvalued exchange rate, which was to the detriment of primary exports and agriculture.

The fact that agriculture was neglected while the internal terms of trade were turned against it induced urban migration, which defied the carrying capacity of urban municipalities. Mass migration was also induced by legislated urban wages that were more than two or three times greater than rural incomes. In addition, higher wages were supplemented by social legislation that improved job security and working conditions (p. 88). Hence urban population growth rates were more than twice the total population growth rates (p. 81). Unemployment was exacerbated by systematically getting prices wrong. Thus, an overvalued exchange rate, duty free capital goods imports, subsidized credit, tied aid, and accelerated depreciation all created the incentive to utilize capital intensive techniques (pp. 86–90).

Balance of payment problems were induced by imports of intermediate and capital goods but dealing with this deficit created perverse incentives. The practice of allocating scarce foreign exchange based on each firm's existing capacity created the perverse incentive of adding to capacity. This practice resulted in the underutilization of capacity since materials and components could not be procured due to foreign exchange scarcity (p. 93). Another perverse incentive created was inducing domestic luxury goods production since protection enhanced incentives for local production (p. 40).[15] The most destructive perverse incentive was the rent-seeking associated with foreign exchange scarcity since it provided higher returns than enterprise; a misallocation of scarce entrepreneurial talent.

Another problem was the scale and range of administrative controls that proliferated in developmentalist states. These various interventions included differential taxes, tax holidays, accelerated depreciation, exemptions, rationing, quotas, price controls, licensing, credit guarantees, subsidized credit, duty free imports, and multiple exchange rates (pp. 35–43). The report concluded that such ponderous controls also produced industries encumbered by sub-optimal firms and high costs. Just as Bauer had noted earlier, this scale of public intervention in economic life resulted in inefficiency and corruption. For many goods, inefficiency caused the value added calculated in world prices to be negative (p. 112).[16]

Not long after the OEDC report was published, the NBER published several books drawing from ten country studies. In these publications, which included Krueger (1977, 1978, 1983) and Bhagwati (1978), ISI and export promotion (EP) were posited as alternative trade and development strategies. EP was declared as preferable since it was associated with more rapid economic growth, unskilled labor intensity and employment (Krueger 1983, pp. 42–43). As also noted by the OECD study, ISI resulted in periodic balance of payment crisis due to the need for importing raw materials, and intermediate and capital goods. Many of these economies rapidly proceeded through the easy phase of ISI, achieving economies of scale by producing consumer goods for relatively poor consumers. But after this, they confronted small market sizes. Overall these economies experienced slower growth rates because capital-output ratios increased incrementally and growth decreased. Also, controls proliferated and became more complex and harmful (pp. 47–48). Regulating production through licensing meant that there was no market weeding of the less efficient firms or privileging of the more efficient ones. By contrast, firms in an EP strategy faced no such constraint. Scale could also be easily achieved since they were not confined to the domestic market and efficiency was induced by the need to compete in the global market (pp. 52–53).

Deepak Lal

Bauer's mantle has been assumed by Deepak Lal, a likeminded free market economist, who berated the interventionist ideology of the developmentalists and Latin structuralists, which he termed *dirigisme*. Elaborating on a point made earlier by Bauer (1957, pp. 14–33) and Bauer and Yamey (1968), Lal contended that because agents in LICs (households and firms) behaved very much as did agents in HICs, regular neo-classical economics was adequate to explain the economics of LICs. Further, he cited evidence to dispute the presence of surplus labor, thus challenging the validity of Lewis's dual economy model (1983, p. 90).[17] More importantly, Lal implied that if there is no surplus labor then trickle down is a fact. Given the inevitability of government failure, Lal argued, "getting prices right" was the best policy.[18]

Structural adjustment and the Washington Concensus

Non-interventionism received a boost during the 1980s Latin American debt crisis, forming the basis for the program of action proposed in the Baker and Brady plans, for which the IMF was a major player. Through the elaboration of these plans the idea of "policy conditionality" gained momentum and the IMF and World Bank linked structural adjustment conditionality to loans received by low and middle income countries. These conditionalities were applied both when countries needed temporary assistance due to balance of payment problems, or when they needed more long term development assistance. The multi-part policy prescriptions that had earlier emerged from empirical critiques of ISI were embraced; thus liberalization and openness to trade, capital flows and foreign investment were enforced, along with privatization and deregulation.

This policy package mentioned above came to be referred to as the "Washington Consensus" or neo-liberalism as it is more pejoratively referred to. The policy program amounted to extending the frontier of the market in economic life and concomitantly pushing back the role of the state. This program has been characterized as an amalgam of neo-classical economics, which provides the intellectual rigor, and the Austrian school, which provides the political and moral philosophy (Chang 2002, p. 540).[19]

Williamson (2008), credited with coining the term "Washington Consensus," points out that this term has acquired meanings not intended by him when he first identified what he viewed the consensus to be in 1989 (Williamson, 1990). He had initially distanced the Washington Consensus from the neo-liberalism of the Mount Pelerin Society or the Reagan-Bush focus on supply side economics, monetarism, and minimal government. The original ten-point consensus he outlined included fiscal discipline, re-ordering public sector priorities (to be pro-growth and pro-poor), tax reform (raising the base and reducing rates), interest rate liberalization, a competitive exchange rate regime, trade liberalization, foreign direct investment liberalization, privatization, deregulation, and expanding property rights.[20]

Summary

Bauer was a scathing and iconoclastic critic of those he disagreed with and a bold defender of liberalism. In assuming the role of dissenter, Bauer often seemed to create straw men.[21] Nonetheless, he had the courage to state what he saw as the truth even while his position might have been viewed as unpopular at the time. For example, he asserted that productivity differences varied by ethnicity (1984, pp. 7–8), that inequality within and across nations could be explained by the lack of "ambition, perceptiveness, resourcefulness and effort" among those that did not prosper (p. 82), and that colonialism was a blessing (p. 58). He also played a valuable role in keeping an alternative liberal perspective on the table when he saw it under siege and its survival at stake (p. 37).

While dissent and criticism constituted much of what he wrote, his unique contribution to development economics was in introducing a theory of development based on notions of liberalism and the associated values of liberty and choice for producers and consumers. By the same token, he pointed out that dirigisme hindered growth due to the associated inefficiency and corruption and this represented his theory of underdevelopment. His writing also contained hints of concepts such as urban bias, rent-seeking and public interest that were more fully fleshed out by subsequent writers.

Bauer's arguments received empirical support in the early 1970s from major case studies commissioned by the OECD and the NBER. These studies suggested that protection and extensive intervention in the economy resulted in inefficiencies, resource misallocation, and corruption. Agriculture and primary exports were systematically discriminated against and industry was privileged, without any empirical justification. The consequent impoverishment of agriculture resulted in migration, unemployment, poverty, and inequality. These findings labeled the ISI project as misconceived, at best. Given the evidence that had come to light on the economic impacts of ISI, its continuation was perceived as malfeasance.

Economists such as Deepak Lal and William Easterly assumed Bauer's mantle and used this and other evidence to support their analytical critique of dirigisme. The debate appeared to resolve itself in favor of a non-interventionist and market oriented approach to economic development that came to be called the Washington Consensus, or, more pejoratively, neo-liberalism. In the early 1990s, however, another set of case studies challenged the non-interventionist approach. These studies and the debates they sparked are reviewed in Chapter 7.

Notes

1 The core economic philosophy that inspired these project/prescriptions remains dominant at the time of writing with some acknowledgements of critics and some accommodations.

2 Bauer acknowledged Yamey, his close friend, colleague, research partner, and co-author, as having greatly contributed to his thinking such that it was difficult to attribute the origin of the ideas in his writings to any one among them. In the early 1970s Bauer was my professorial advisor and Yamey my teacher, a truly outstanding one, at the London School of Economics.

3 As commonly understood, the difference between the two perspectives is "freedom from" deprivations, as Sen defines development, and "freedom to" be full market actors in the libertarian tradition, as Bauer and Yamey defined development. There is an overlap in that Sen includes access to exchange on the market as among fundamental freedoms (refer to Chapter 5).

4 Unlike the classical scholars and developmentalists, Bauer and Yamey viewed capital accumulation as endogenous (p. 127).

5 Bauer and Yamey seem to be setting up a straw man here since the developmentalists preferred private sector activity and advocated state owned enterprises only on a temporary basis and only in activities that the private sector avoided due to various market failures.

6 This theme of urban bias was later developed by Lipton (1977).

7 This theme of rent-seeking was later developed by Krueger (1974).

8 They were as justified in making these assertions as were the developmentalists in making their counter-assertions. Since neither provided evidence of the form currently acceptable, the issue at that point in the debate was to be resolved by economic logic.

9 Here the authors open themselves to the usual criticism that if the state has the competence to collect and disseminate appropriate information, they may have the competence to engage in other activities also.

10 While Bauer cites Smith often, the latter's key insight regarding the much greater labor productivity inherent in industry (Chapter 1) is not one Bauer shared.

11 Unlike Nurkse who thought that imported luxury consumption goods could dissipate savings for capital accumulation, Bauer (1957, pp. 66–67) thought that such goods could stimulate economic activity to create the income for purchase of such goods.

12 Bauer's work on traders anticipated the literature in development economics on the informal sector, a claim he made in later writing. Lewis is normally credited for the use of this term in the context of it being a reservoir for surplus labor.

13 Bauer made the same argument regarding vicious circles i.e. if currently rich countries did not experience them, there is no reason for the poor countries to do so. However, there is an implicit assumption here that the initial conditions were the same. Refer to Myrdal (1956, p. 170) on differing initial conditions for developed and underdeveloped countries.

14 Kay (1989, p. 39) pointed out that ECLA, credited with initiating ISI in Latin America under Prebish's leadership (see Chapter 2), had begun to criticize ISI in the 1950s for being too capital intensive, for having limited scale economies potential, and for generating unemployment and inequality.

15 Recall that Furtado (Chapter 4) had made the same criticisms about possible perverse incentives in the industrialization process.

16 Negative value added is one reason that the effective protection rates (ERP), defined as value added at domestic prices minus value added at world prices to the base of value added at world prices, were found to be negative. The other reason was that there was more protection for inputs than final goods, suggesting a non-rationalized tariff structure. If the value added at world prices was small, the ERP could be astronomical. For a critique of this tool refer to Fine (2005, chapter 4).

17 This debate has continued and Rosenzweig and Foster (2010) estimated surplus labor in Indian agriculture of over 20 percent on farm sizes of 20 acres or less.

18 Easterly (2002, 2006) has popularized many of these ideas. The 2002 book contains a useful chapter on the negative impact of ethnicity on economic growth. This was an issue Myrdal (1956) was very concerned about since he viewed the lack of national integration as one of the main obstacles to development since it could induce negative cumulative causation and development as one of the key solutions to national integration in terms of inducing positive cumulative causation (see Chapter 4).

19 Calclough (1991, pp. 17–22) argues that neo-liberals are more likely to engage in policy advocacy than neo-classical economists.

20 In does seem, however, that the strong emphasis on privatization, liberalization, and deregulation of this program is suggestive of minimal government.
21 For example, he viewed virtually the whole development profession as supportive of foreign aid though this was certainly not true for the developmentalist pioneers reviewed in Chapter 2; only Rosenstein-Rodan made a case for foreign capital to initiate development. Only as a business proposition Hirschman conceded that it may have a role but only after the development momentum was underway, and Nurkse and Lewis emphasized domestic resource mobilization.

References

Bauer, P. T. 1984. *Reality and Rhetoric: Studies in the Economics of Development*. Cambridge, Mass.: Harvard University Press.

Bauer, P. T. 1972. *Dissent on Development*. Cambridge, Mass.: Harvard University Press.

Bauer, P. T. 1957. *Economic Analysis and Policy in Underdeveloped Countries*. Durham, N. C.: Duke University Press.

Bauer, P. T. and Yamey, B. S. 1968. *Markets, Market Control and Marketing Reform*. London: Weidenfeld and Nicolson.

Bauer, P. T. and Yamey, B. S. 1957. *The Economics of Under-Developed Countries*. Chicago: The University of Chicago Press.

Bhagwati, J. 1978. *Anatomy and Consequences of Exchange Control Regimes*. Cambridge: Ballinger Press.

Calclough. C. 1991. "Structuralism vs. Neo-Liberalism." In: C. Calclough and J. Manor, eds., *States or Markets? Neo-Liberalism and the Development Policy Debates*. Oxford: Clarendon Press.

Chang, H.-J. 2002. "Breaking the Mould: An Institutionalist Political Economy Alternative to the Neo-Liberal Theory of the Market and the State." *Cambridge Journal of Economics*, 26 (5), 539–559.

Easterly, W. 2006. *The White Man's Burden: Why the West's Efforts to Aid the Rest Have Done So Much Ill and So Little Good*. New York: Penguin Books.

Easterly, W. 2002. *The Elusive Quest for Growth: Economists' Adventures and Misadventures in the Tropics*. Cambridge, Massachusetts: MIT Press.

Fine, B. 2005. "The Development State and Political Economy of Development." In B. Fine and K. S. Jomo, eds., *The New Development Economics: Post Washington Consensus Neo-Liberal Thinking*. London: Zed Books.

Rosenzweig, M. and Foster, A. D. 2010. "Is There Surplus Labor in Rural India?" Yale Growth Center, Working Paper No. 85. New Haven.

Grabel, I. 2010. "Cementing Neo-Liberalism in the Developing World: Ideational and Institutional Constraints on Policy Space." In: S. R. Khan and J. Christiansen, eds., *Market as Means Rather than Master: Towards New Developmentalism*. London: Routledge.

Kay, C. 1989. *Latin American Theories of Development and Underdevelopment*. London: Routledge.

Krueger, A. 1983. *Trade and Employment in Developing Countries, Vol. 3: Synthesis and Conclusions*. Chicago: University of Chicago Press.

Krueger, A. 1978. *Foreign Trade Regimes and Economic Development: Liberalization Attempts and Consequences*. Cambridge: Ballenger Press.

Krueger, A. 1977. "Growth, distortions and patterns of trade among many countries," *Princeton Studies in International Finance*, No 40. Princeton, New Jersey: Princeton University Press.

Krueger, A. 1974. "The Political Economy of the Rent Seeking Society." *American Economic Review*, 64 (3), 291–303.

Lal, D. 1983. *The Poverty of Development Economics*. Cambridge, Massachusetts.: Harvard University Press.

Lipton, M. 1977. *Why Poor People Stay Poor: Urban Bias in World Development*. Cambridge, Mass.: Harvard University Press.

Little, I., Scitovsky, T., and Scott, M. 1970. *Industry and Trade in Some Developing Countries*. Oxford: Oxford University Press for the OECD Development Center.

Myrdal, G. 1956. *An International Economy*. New York: Harper & Brothers Publishers.

Williamson, J. 2008. "A Short History of the Washington Consensus." In: N. Serra and J. E. Stiglitz, eds., *The Washington Consensus Reconsidered: Towards a New Global Governance*. New York: Oxford University Press.

Williamson, J. 1990. "What Washington Means by Policy Reform." In: *Latin American adjustment. How much has happened?* In: John Williamson, ed., Washington, D.C.: Institute for International Economics, 7–33.

Part IV
Neo-liberalism challenged

7 Developmentalist resurgence

Introduction[1]

Developmentalism or structuralism[2] resurfaced in the 1980s and 1990s to challenge the neo-liberal interpretation of why countries like Japan, South Korea and Taiwan, China developed when they did and proffered industrial policy as an alternative policy agenda to structural adjustment. Industry is viewed by developmentalists as special (see Chapter 2) because unlike other sectors it is subject to increasing returns, technological learning, and skill acquisition that result in productivity increase and higher wages. Industrial policy is defined as an attempt by the state to strategically influence targeted industries.[3] The essence of successful policy is not "picking winners," but creating winners based on the track record of developed countries.[4] Effective industrial policy thus became a core element of developmentalism, just as structural adjustment was, and arguably still is, the core element of neo-liberalism.[5] Just as structural adjustment is a broad program industrial policy entails the implementation of supportive policies addressing trade, technology, employment, finance, infrastructure, competition, and institutions.

As with the early developmentalists, the trade theory underpinning of developmentalism is still dynamic comparative advantage: that engaging in high-value industrial activities would yield technological development, learning by doing, training, labor productivity, income-elasticity, economies of scale, energy efficiency, and externalities (including diffusing managerial and marketing skills) which lead to increasing returns and justify product selection and specialization regardless of "inherent" or current comparative advantage.

Contemporary developmentalist scholars have established the role of the state as important, assuming a reasonably efficient economic bureaucracy. This came as an important challenge to the neo-liberal agenda of rolling back the state based on an assumption of "government failure" (see Chapter 6). Current structuralists or developmentalists point out that "good government" is just as fundamental for implementing neo-liberal structural adjustment as for implementing industrial policy programs. The commonality among contemporary developmentalist scholars is their eclecticism, pragmatism, and support of institutional development and all agree that the market should be harnessed as a mere means for development.[6]

How do contemporary developmentalists differ from their predecessors? The vision of sustained economic development is the same—it is conceived as a process centered on industrialization, diversification, and moving to higher value added activities based on acquiring an indigenous technological capacity. While the early developmentalists relied on conceptual arguments, contemporary dev-leopmentalists have based their arguments on careful and painstaking case studies that present an alternative to the OECD and NBER research projects which provided evidence to refute developmentalism. In a nutshell, these altern-ative studies argue that the developmentalist vision has in fact been realized by several states in the race for global economic advancement. In other words, there is evidence that ISI can be done right despite the fact that getting it right is a demanding institutional challenge.

While there were differences among the countries researched, the commonal-ity was their coherent, nuanced, and well-implemented industrial and support policies. This observation came as a challenge to the mainstream view that suc-cessful development was the result of free market policies. Establishing an alternative explanation was a significant landmark in the economic development literature, one that the World Bank has acknowledged (World Bank, 2005).[7]

Many additions and conceptual refinements have been made to early develop-mentalist thinking based on case studies of East and Southeast Asian Newly Industrialized Countries (NICs). The operational design principles include the following: First, a combination of incentives (carrots) and performance criteria (stick) were used to ensure business success in selected activities.[8] Thus, con-tinued incentives/subsidies were based on a firm's ability to show local content use, profit growth, and productivity growth and quality identified by breaking into export markets.[9] The selection of activities has gone beyond linkages identi-fied by Hirschman (Chapter 2) to a number of other criteria reviewed below in detail. Third, the government determined the optimal number of players in an industry in order to preserve both competition and economies of scale, thus ensuring internal market competition even as they sought to protect firms from premature external competition.[10] Fourth, to create the rents necessary to induce activity, the state needs to try to get the incentives right, which is not the same as getting prices right.[11] Finally, ISI and export promotion (EP) have a symbiotic association and are not alternative strategies. ISI is viewed as necessary to build a base for EP, which in turn provides resources (particularly foreign exchange) to further ISI in other industries, thereby propelling the economy up the value chain. Thus, while some industries may be going through an ISI phase, others may have graduated to EP.

These principles suggest that developmentalism is as much a theory of gov-ernment as a set of economic development policies. For developmentalists, poverty is merely a symptom of the failure to generate sustainable, high quality jobs in increasing returns industrial activities. Since jobs are the focus, this approach differs from the compartmentalization of neo-liberalism, whereby structural adjustment creates poverty and poverty alleviation programs address the fallout.[12] It also differs from the human development approach of the

Millennium Development Goals (MDG), which Chang (2010b) views as a band aid strategy or false development since the focus is not on the nature of production and jobs as the central aspect of development.

Key thinkers

Chalmers Johnson, Alice Amsden (1944–2012), Robert Wade, and Ha-Joon Chang are key thinkers whose seminal works are reviewed in this section.[13] They all used a historical approach with much detailed attention to the evolution of institutions. The three countries they studied, Japan, South Korea, and Taiwan, all demonstrated good leadership at a critical period to induce unparallel catch-up growth. In Japan and South Korea's case, this leadership was motivated by a strong sense of patriotism and nationhood. In South Korea, a strong security imperative also played a role, as it did in Taiwan. I have abstracted from the economic and institutional history to focus on key design principles emanating from the rich work of these authors.

Chalmers Johnson (1931–2010)

Johnson's *MITI and the Japanese Miracle* (1982) was a key study that contributed to initiating the developmentalist resurgence. He pointed out that the defining characteristic of the Japanese economic system during its transition to high income status in the 1960s, formerly marked by its joining the OECD (Organization of Economic Cooperation and Development) in 1964, was the collaboration between the state and big business. Specifically, this centered on the execution of industrial policy by the Ministry of International Trade and Industry (MITI).[14] MITI drew from the country's top universities like the University of Tokyo and was thus staffed by the most talented (p. 20). The bureaucracy "ruled" and MITI, for example, was able to execute industrial policy at will while the parliament (Diet) reigned and often ran interference if there was public disaffection (p. 315). The social consensus for developmentalism in Japan was honed by the hardships experienced by the population in the 1930s and 1940s and by the income leveling effect of the war and post-war inflation (p. 307). The social purpose of this egalitarianism was recognized and preserved such that the gap in private living standards of top executives and ordinary workers were not very large even in the 1970s (p. 314).

Several social institutions that had evolved over time to address various historical circumstances were tapped to attain high speed growth. The lack of social safety nets, large bi-annual lump-sum bonuses, housing and land shortages, and a poorly developed consumer credit system induced high saving rates, which the government mobilized via postal accounts by paying competitive interest rates and exempting the interest earnings from taxes (p. 14). The "three sacred treasures," namely traditional enterprise unions, seniority based wages and "lifetime" employment created labor-capital harmony, innovation (including labor saving ones), a focus on quality control, and product development timed to market demand. (p. 11).

Lifetime employment meant a measure of job security, but in downturns senior staff were the first to be pensioned or retrained since they were the most expensive. The dual labor market, which provided a large proportion of temporary employees (up to two-fifths for Toyota), and supply sub-contracting provided a cushion for employers in downturns. Temporary employees were first to be let go in downturns and large corporations squeezed sub-contractors (p. 12). Similarly, the distribution system with a ratio of wholesale to retail of 4.8/1 compared to 1.3/1 in the US absorbed labor. Japan also used a high employment policy and low taxes as cheaper alternatives to instituting unemployment insurance (p. 13).

The discretionary power of the bureaucracy was such that the Diet simply rubber stamped its budget so that "appropriations precede authorization." In this regard, MITI's powers derived from a "second budget" i.e. the Fiscal Investment and Loan Plan (FILP) which amounted to a sizable 3.3 percent (1956) to 6.3 percent (1972) of GDP with funds mobilized from postal savings. In addition, it controlled the Export-Import Bank and the Japanese Development Bank (JDB). Even when its ability to shape incentives by controlling finance was less of an issue in absolute terms in the 1970s, an MITI-approved JDB loan constituted a seal of approval which made it easier for a corporation to secure private financing (pp. 208–211).

The success of Japan's industrial policy was ensured by various institutional practices that promoted state-business sector partnership. A prominent example was "descent from heaven," whereby senior bureaucrats retired into prominent positions in corporations, often the ones they had managed as part of the vertical MITI structure for industrial policy oversight (p. 70). This ensured a common understanding between representatives of the MITI and business by ensuring that both junior bureaucrats and senior ex-bureaucrats were prominent parties in the deliberation councils where policy formation was discussed. MITI had 38 deliberation councils and again the Diet rubber-stamped recommendations (p. 48). In addition, there were formal discussion groups including public and private officials and the exchange of officials between the state and private enterprise (p. 312). Common understanding and purpose was also cemented by the fact that many ex-bureaucrats became influential politicians, even attaining the top office of prime minister (p. 46).

Apart from its control of finance, MITI relied on several other tools and economic institutions to ensure that its "guidance" would be followed and its plans realized. Most importantly, it determined scarce foreign exchange allocations and also influenced tax policy to shape incentives. Foreign exchange allocations, rather than tariffs, were the most significant tool for controlling imports and protecting strategic industries. Responsive businesses, in terms of MITI's industrial policy goals, were able to get credit on easier terms, licenses, duty relaxations, tax breaks, protection, foreign exchange, and approval for joint ventures for the transfer of technology (pp. 25, 29).

Johnson argued that securing advanced technology "was the heart of the matter" (p. 16). From 1950 to 1980, the Foreign Capital Law enabled MITI to approve all joint ventures and technology transfer via licensing (p. 17). It aggressively negotiated and leaned on foreign companies to sell technology on favorable terms and limited their domestic sales (pp. 247, 28). Subsidies were provided for experimental installation and trial of new machines and equipment and additional incentives were rapid amortization and local tax exempted for R&D expenditures (p. 218). With its clout and cooperative business relations, MITI ensured the diffusion of best practice.

MITI also ensured that the broader economic environment was enabling. Demand-creation was attained not only with protection but also with consumer credit and tax incentives. Alternatively, when the domestic market was saturated, tax incentives were provided for exports. Central and local governments also facilitated industrial policy by building ports, highways, railroads, electric power grids, gas mains, and industrial parks.

MITI ensured that there was competition, but not overcompetition. It was important that economies of scale were realized and MITI ensured the optimum number of players in an industry for this purpose using enforced mergers if need be. Small and medium sized enterprises were sometimes urged to move into other activities using sweeteners like loans and tax breaks. The desired market structure was then preserved by blocking entry and setting investment rates (p. 256). Vertical industry bureaus in MITI were able to engage in such micromanagement although the task was not easy since corporations were keen to be included in a government guaranteed industry (pp. 206–207). Sony and Honda are celebrated examples of corporations that proceeded despite MITI guidance.[15]

The conglomerate structure of large Japanese business houses (*keiretsu*) included a big bank, several industrial firms and a general trading company with cross stock ownerships. The bank drew on MITI facilitated finance, allowing the firms to focus on long term objectives such as product development, quality control and foreign market penetration (p. 204). The trading companies supplied raw materials on credit and fiercely promoted exports when the domestic market was exhausted (p. 205).

The oligopolistic or monopolistically competitive market structure also enabled MITI to induce cooperative behavior when needed. This included sharing technology, limiting product lines, joint use of warehouses, and joint consultations on investment strategies (p. 225). Such an industrial structure also enabled MITI to nudge industries to diversify into products with a high income elasticity of demand and high productivity, such as heavy and chemical industries. Consequently, Japan was able to move up the value chain and to offset a persistent balance of payment deficit (p. 228). If the business in question was too risky or the capital cost too high for private enterprise, MITI created a public-private corporation to initiate industries and fed them into the economy when deemed ready for commercialization. There were 115 such partnerships forged in industries such as synthetic rubber and textiles, plastics, petrochemicals, automobiles, and electronics (pp. 313, 237).

Eventually, success and prosperity forced MITI out of its interventionism. Joining the OECD, IMF, and GATT exposed Japan to external pressures to liberalize the economy—including trade and foreign investment—in order to harmonize with the club of rich countries. Even MITI could not overcome these pressures. Previously, in the 1950s, Japan had successfully ensured institutional continuity by resisting or bypassing the very powerful occupation authority (Supreme Commander of the Allied Powers—SCAP) (p. 41). For example, when the *zaibatsu* were abolished, MITI had nurtured the *keiretsu*, which had a similar conglomerate bank financing structure even though the family ownership was no longer as predominant. But Japan was in a new era in the 1970s.

New prosperity meant new challenges and opportunities. Overcrowding due to rural-urban migration and environmental degradation were getting the public's attention. There was a need to move to smokeless and knowledge intensive higher value added industries (for example integrated circuit machines, computers, robotics, high fashion including furniture, high-value services in consulting and management, systems engineering, and software) (p. 291). What worked in the 1950s with vertical industry bureaus was no longer suitable for an already industrialized economy. The next generation of leadership with an understanding of the new industries and mode of operating moved into place (p. 309). Administrative guidance including directives, requests, suggestions, encouragements, and warnings took the place of explicit control (p. 265).

Reading the narrative above may create the impression of an infallible economic bureaucracy that had it all worked out and then went about effectively executing a patriotic vision. Johnson points out that this was not how it worked: Instead, through trial and error, hard work, and some luck, a system evolved to meet economic challenges and attain high-speed growth. The process was dynamic and the tools used varied depending on the economy's needs (p. 29). Along the way, the bureaucracy often overreached and faced business resentment since, like businesses anywhere, Japanese firms preferred self-governance. The economic bureaucracy also engaged in fierce turf battles like bureaucracies anywhere and faced public approbation over mostly minor corruption scandals that were inevitable given the power they were able to concentrate. But overall, there was little doubt that MITI worked for the public good and that in this regard it was judged to be very effective.

Alice Amsden (1944–2012)

Amsden's case study, *Asia's Next Giant* (1989), documented and explained South Korea's economic catch-up growth. General Park Chung-hee modeled South Korea after Japan viewing nationalistic patriotism to be the basis of the Meiji reform and economic growth, which during his term in office averaged between 9 and 10 percent (p. 55). By 1960, prior to General Park Chung-hee's takeover in 1961, unemployment was estimated to be 20 percent and South Korea had a per capita GDP of less than $100, roughly the same as that of India (p. 46). By 1996, South Korea joined the OECD.

Amsden framed her work as a study of late industrialization.[16] She identified "learning" as the mechanism used by later industrializers, given the backlog of available technologies. This contrasted with other drivers of industrialization, such as invention in the case of Great Britain, and innovation in the case of the USA (p. 4). What enabled learning to happen was an interventionist state with appropriate support institutions, an abundant supply of engineers (as gatekeepers of foreign technology), salaried managers, a well-educated labor force, and diversified business conglomerates (known as *chaebols*).

Chaebols were the counterpart of the Japanese *keiretsu*. By 1984, the three largest ones represented 36 percent of GNP (p. 116). The state limited entry into an industry to ensure economies of scale and effective diversification (economies of scope). It was, however, intensely committed to the concept of competition that prevailed in Japan (pp. 17, 136). While protected from external competition in the initial stages of new manufacturing activity, *chaebols* competed fiercely for favors from the state based on delivering good economic performance, product innovation, quality, and exports. To attain these objectives, there was also intense competition to acquire foreign technology on the best terms, the best personnel, and customers (p. 116).

The military's method of dealing with illegal wealth accumulation during the tenure of the Syngman Rhee (1948–1960) administration became the basis for an alliance of big business and the state. Businesses were exempted from criminal prosecution and from the confiscation of property in exchange for their efforts to establish new industrial firms in basic industries. Businesses that delivered on economic objectives, particularly exports, could count on state support (p. 72). Yet, while this quid pro quo method persisted, the partnership was unequal and there was no question about who was in charge. For example, given the central role of foreign exchange in the industrialization project, capital flight was punishable by jail sentences with the death sentence as the maximum penalty (p. 17).

The *chaebols* facilitated the move from light to heavy industry (p. 20). They used various mechanisms for technology transfer: international expositions, conferences, technology journals, visits to overseas plants and machinery suppliers, and anything else that would allow them to "beg, borrow or steal foreign designs." When necessary, technical assistance and licenses were purchased and this was considered preferable to relying on foreign direct investment (p. 20). This ensured industrialization was premised on national enterprise with FDI amounting to at most 5 percent of GDP (p. 76).

In the mid 1980s, the government was still driving industrial change and pushing industrialists into high value added industries such as electronics. Incentives included subsidies, the formation of industrial estates and industry-specific research institutes for R&D, and public-private joint ventures for research, infrastructure spending, and trade protection (pp. 81–82, 328–329).[17] Public sector companies were established only when the private sector was not forthcoming because incentives were outweighed by high gestation period, perceived risk, or low expected returns. In such cases, public sector companies were turned over to the private sector after a period of public-private partnership once the *chaebols* gained more experience (p. 88). In justifying intervention, Amsden argues that there is little reason to believe that the free market would necessarily create the optimum level and kind of investment since ultimately the outcome is premised on business preferences—taste for risk (p. 100). Planning gave the government an overview and a better sense of the nature of diversification needed (p. 84).

What distinguished the state from others in Latin America or Asia was its ability to implement reciprocity; performance standards were granted in exchange of various kinds of subsidies including licenses to invest (pp. 8, 146). These reciprocal subsidies included preferential loans for facility expansion and research and development, tax and tariff exemptions, and wastage allowances, in addition to support for overheads (pp. 63–68). Beyond making working capital available to all exporters, the nationalized banking system provided particularly favorable rates to firms in targeted industries (p. 73).

As earlier indicated, performance was judged in terms of the ability to export, and to produce new products through successful R&D. Good performance was rewarded, while poor performance was penalized. Badly managed *chaebols* were dismantled even if it meant abandoning "friends" of the regime. When *chaebols* were dissolved, other regime allies were allowed to take over extra capacity, but had to justify the favor with good performance (p. 16). However, while the state penalized poor performance, during crisis conditions the state's response was to facilitate corporate borrowing (at negative interest rates based on its exchange rate policy) to bail out companies rather than move to austerity (pp. 94, 105).

Although unionization was repressed, workers' wages rose rapidly from a low base due to government pressure. This was done to attain a number of objectives including sharing wealth with labor for social stability, a larger market, inducing productivity and technology acquisition, and an incentive/reward for workers to learn to operate this technology (pp. 146, 189). Much of South Korea's productivity growth came from the intensive shop floor level experience based on the "quality circle" practice learnt from the Japanese (pp. 5, 251–252). Thus, labor played a big role in catch-up development.

In the initial stages of the industrialization drive, social expenditure was very limited and the middle class was taxed for resource mobilization (p. 18, p. 92). To create profitable opportunities for desired industries the state deliberately "got prices wrong" (p. 14). Even after banks were privatized due to US pressure, the state retained effective control of commercial banks.

Reflecting on the developmentalist model that South Korea used, Amsden posits that growth theory is not sufficient to explain South Korea's development. While growth theory posits that causality runs from higher productivity to enhanced growth, the South Korean model suggests that growth itself very likely enables acquisition of technology, scale economies and learning by doing. Thus, instead of a unidirectional causality, there is a virtuous cycle whereby growth enables greater productivity, which yields higher growth (pp. 109–112).[18]

She also points to a conundrum the implementation of developmentalism faces: Implementing developmentalist prescriptions required a strong state, such as the one that emerged in South Korea for various historical and institutional reasons. But countries often experience underdevelopment precisely because

they have weak states (p. 142). Getting rid of price distortions is politically difficult because it hurts vested interests. Thus, as she points out, "getting prices
right" is just as contingent on a strong state as "getting prices wrong."[19]

In *The Rise of the Rest* (2001) Amsden pursued the theme of late industrialization and how it is based on knowledge as the "most precious of all assets"
(p. iii). Departing from the neo-classical assumption of perfect information,
Amsden claims that knowledge is painstakingly acquired from "pure learning."
It is different from information in that it is conceptual, tacit, experience based,
and firm specific. Given the firm specific nature of knowledge, technology
cannot be codified while information can be, and it is (p. 5).

Amsden's inductive study of this issue included Argentina, Brazil, Chile,
India, Mexico, South Korea, Taiwan, Thailand, and Turkey. The commonality in
these developmentalist states, with the exception of Argentina, was "getting
prices wrong" and institutions and "control mechanisms" to implement reciprocity right. She documented the catch-up economic development history of these
cases and demonstrated how structural factors like manufacturing experience
and equality led to different trajectories. The developmentalist states used the
mechanisms of development banking, infrastructure construction, local-content
management, the public sector rather than FDI for technology acquisition, and
selective protection in their catch-up process (p. 126). Taiwan, for example,
premised protection on saving foreign exchange, maximizing linkages, export
market potential and high technology, value added and energy intensity and low
pollution intensity (pp. 136–137).[20]

All the developmentalist states managed with varying success to move from
buying to making technology although the "independents" that relied on R&D
and innovation systems, such as South Korea and Taiwan, were more successful
than the "integrationists" like Brazil and Mexico that relied on FDI with the
onset of the liberal economic order (pp. 238–245). She cited evidence to show
that the developmentalist states managed to create industries that withstood the
pressure of market competition when they had to liberalize and that dynamic
comparative advantage was realized in industries such as electrical and non-
electrical manufacturing and transportation equipment (pp. 260–268). There
were no dramatic structural changes after liberalization and the identified
selected leading industries yielded dramatic future growth.

Notwithstanding the liberalization ushered in with the WTO regime in 1995,
Amsden explored the specific binding clauses and showed that "the liberal bark
of the WTO appeared to be worse than its bite" (pp. 268–271). Thus she argued
that there was adequate policy space for developmentalism although, given the
nature of permissible subsidies, the focus would need to be on R&D rather than
export promotion. The most interesting country comparison is that between
Chile, which in 1973 embarked on a state led model focusing on the primary
sub-sectors of mining and agro-industries, and Taiwan, which continued on the
path of developing knowledge based assets in manufacturing. In 1973 Taiwan's
per capita GDP was a fraction of Chile's (73 percent), but by 1995 Chile's per
capita GDP was a similar fraction of Taiwan's (68 percent) (p. 291).

Escape from Empire (2008) covered many of the same themes identified above for a more general audience.[21] Here, Amsden pointed out that for historical (a partly self-interested anti-colonial stand) and political reasons (anti-communism) the US tolerated developmentalism in low and middle income countries. However, Japan's challenge to US manufacturing was a wake-up call with regards to the threat that this mode of catch-up development posed. Since the 1980s, then, the US has championed neo-liberalism (see Chapter 6), which serves the interests of US capital (both Wall Street and MNCs) by pushing liberalization, privatization, and deregulation, and which represents an assault on the developmental state (pp. 13–14, 128). Wage repression in LICs became the norm with a subsequent swelling of the informal sector (pp. 134–135).

Robert Wade

Robert Wade's tour de force is *Governing the Market* (2004), a case study of how Taiwan managed to initiate catch-up development.[22] Wade's training in politics and anthropology as well as in economics makes the book particularly rich and insightful. He argues that neo-classical prescriptions amount to a free market or simulated market approach (neutral incentives for domestic and export production). According to Wade, a balanced review of the evidence suggests that neo-liberal policies are reasonable explanations for Taiwan's catch-up growth given its export orientation, low financial repression, high saving and investment rates, budget surpluses, seemingly competitive industrial structure, a well-trained labor force, wages at market clearing levels, and a stable political environment. However, this suggests an "identification problem" since closer inspection also reveals a highly interventionist state. Wade proposes that Taiwan "governed the market," but that neo-classical economists paid little attention to evidence consistent with this claim (pp. 71–72). Focusing on Taiwan, he goes on to explore how the East Asian economies successfully used a market governing approach to attain high catch-up growth rates.

Catch-up growth in Taiwan preceded South Korea by a decade or so, and was just as impressive. Real GDP grew at an average of 8.8 percent between 1953 and 1986. This was accompanied by an unusually equal distribution of income. Real earnings increased by 18 percent between 1960 and 1980, even while unionization was repressed. Also during roughly this period (1968 to 1982), unemployment was halved from the already low 4 percent at the beginning of the period. By 1979, it was the largest exporter of manufactured exports to the OECD including electronic goods such as calculators, car parts, cassette recorders, personal computers, and machine tools. Thus the material conditions of life were transformed within one generation (p. 138).

The ideal of social equality and the symbiotic relationship of agriculture and industry that Lewis had recommended (chapter 2) were advanced in Taiwan, as in South Korea, by Japanese land reforms that ended absentee ownership and transferred land to local smallholders. The Japanese provided fertilizer and manure to boost rice and sugar production for their own needs (p. 73).

Post-World War II, the "mainlanders" (from Mainland China) instituted another round of land reforms, invested in irrigation and rural infrastructure, and provided smallholders with inputs at subsidized rates. This enabled the state to turn the internal terms of trade against agriculture and also draw off the agricultural surplus with taxation (25 percent tax burden) for industrialization (p. 76). The state also encouraged industrialization by blocking other means of wealth accumulation such as land speculation (via the land reform) or financial activity (via bank nationalization and limited financial market development) (pp. 301–302).

Also, as in South Korea, Taiwan inherited a manufacturing base from the Japanese, who relied more on Taiwan as domestic wages rose. Taiwan built on this industrial base using initially overvalued and multiple exchange rates (to favor the public sector), quantitative restrictions, tariffs, and other protective tools (p. 77). But protection was timed and infants had to grow up. Moreover, those not delivering quality had to suffer the consequences including by facing import liberalization (p. 132).

Strong import substitution industrialization was followed by export expansion (p. 84). While, as conventionally defined, Taiwan had an open economy, the government used trade policy to promote certain sectors, raise revenue, and reduce deficits. Import protection was, however, offset by export incentives including an undervalued currency (p. 113). Scarce foreign exchange was allocated based on export performance. Duties on imported inputs for exports were rebated and exporters, who got concessional credit, were allowed to retain foreign exchange earned for import needs (p. 78). Exporting was also facilitated with bonded warehouses, Export Processing Zones (EPZs), quality control with inspections and lab tests (about 50 labs were involved), prizes, export cartel formation, and marketing information (pp. 139–144). Taiwan's China External Trade Development Council with a staff of about 500 maintained 42 overseas offices by 1983. It conducted market research, provided detailed information, and organized participation in trade fairs (pp. 145–148). In general, the state led the market and acted in anticipation of a change in comparative advantage. (p. 110). For example, the move to heavy and chemical and other high technology industries preceded the exhaustion of labor surplus (p. 303).

The state established strategic upstream industries (glass, plastics, steel, cement, chemicals, fertilizer, metal working, food processing, mining, and utilities) and ran them as public enterprises or handed them over to selected private entrepreneurs. Excessive competition was deterred by entry restrictions. However, the state retained control of the "commanding heights" of the economy (petroleum refining, petrochemicals, fertilizer, heavy machinery, trucks, shipbuilding, transport equipment, integrated circuits, metals, gas, water, railways, and utilities) (p. 179). Public enterprises incurred an operating surplus and contributed about 10 percent of government revenue (p. 160). Throughout the 1950s, public enterprises contributed half of industrial output (p. 78). Over time, the public share declined and in 1990 it was down to about a fifth (p. 88).

Credit was directed and state owned banks received a list of industries (six to 12) for priority attention. Loan guarantees were provided and special purpose funds were established such as for machinery imports (pp. 167–170). Tax incentives such as accelerated depreciation, tax holidays, investment credits, and duty free imports of capital goods were earned and retained by good performance. Using domestic content, upgrading technology, cost reduction and exporting were all rewarded in these ways (p. 182).

In strategic industries many firms qualified for incentives while in many other industries only a few firms qualified. In selecting industries to support, planners took into account demand elasticities, trends in technological change and export potential, along with engineering feasibility (given the high incidence of engineers among planners) (p. 188). Economists with a focus on short term efficiency were excluded from this process (pp. 225–226).

Technology was central to the catch-up growth strategy in Taiwan, as in other East Asian economies. One key mechanism for procuring foreign technology was via joint ownership with the foreign companies identified by the state and the terms of partnership emphasizing local content. Alternatively, the state approved the terms of a licensing agreement (pp. 91, 94). Several industry specific research institutes were established and incentives provided for R&D in favored sectors like machine tools, semi-conductors, computers, telecommunications, robotics, and bio-technology. The Industrial Technology Research Institute had a staff size of 4,500 and it worked closely with the Hsin-chu Science Industrial Park with the goal of attaining endogenous technological capacity (p. 98). The Electronics Research and Service Organization had a staff size of 1,700 and engaged in R&D in the information technology sector, using reverse engineering to identify which technologies to acquire. These technologies were then sub-licensed to a relevant firm (pp. 107–108).

Tax credits were provided to firms for R&D as long as the spending was over the average for the last five years and above some minimum threshold level. High technology firms received a credit of 20 percent of annual taxable income. The state also contributed half the R&D expenses and firms could retain profits up to double the paid in capital. Cost sharing was also provided for the acquisition of approved financial and managerial systems. Acquisition of patent rights could amount to a quarter of the equity share and foreign firms were able to get tax exemption by furnishing approved patent rights (p. 185).

To maintain macroeconomic stability, foreign portfolio investment was not allowed except via unit trusts. Foreign capital was prohibited from making purchases on the local stock exchange. Outward foreign investment was subject to state approval based on benefits to the local economy (p. 156). Foreign direct investment in banking was only allowed in pockets of business that locals could not do well (p. 161).

While expenditures on health, welfare, and social security were small in Taiwan, as in South Korea and Japan, education received a share of GDP that rose rapidly from 11.6 percent in 1955–1956 to 20.5 percent in 1970–1971 (p. 174). Within tertiary education, engineering increased from a quarter of enrollments in 1955–1956 to almost a third in 1985–1986 based on manpower planning. Over half the students (55 percent) at the tertiary level were in vocational colleges (p. 190). The state supported higher education abroad, but lost most of the students to the brain drain. Subsequently, with concerted effort, it converted this drain into a brain bank (p. 199).

Taiwan certainly benefited from US strategic interest in the country. At its peak, US aid represented 6 percent of GDP in the 1950s and 40 percent of gross investment. In addition, Taiwan benefited from US technical assistance (pp. 82–85). However, it still deserves credit for making the most of an opportunity that many other low income countries were unable to. Wade considers the question of replication in detail and suggests that the specific political, social, and historic context of each country in East Asia determined its path.[23] However, there are certain design principles all East Asian countries shared and all LICs could learn from.

The products to specialize in are the ones that lend themselves to high growth potential because the expected income elasticity of demand is high or they embody a high potential for technological learning and labor productivity growth. This would apply to capital goods production (p. 357). Wade challenges Bauer's assumption that if profitable opportunities exist, they will find funding. Wade argues that in reality, equity, insurance, and credit markets are often weak or missing and that until they strengthen, government development funding is necessary as the second-best option (p. 353). Bank-based financing is recommended since retained earnings are often inadequate in the beginning, and securities markets can be slow to develop. In any case, security markets often take a short term view, while directed credit can support targeted activities using a long term decision making framework (p. 364). Socializing risk in this way can also give the state leverage for productive restructuring, if required. (p. 367).

Wade challenges the neo-liberal presumption by arguing that ISI and EP are not distinct but rather complementary trade and industrialization strategies.[24] EP provides the necessary foreign exchange for goods at an earlier stage of learning and, once the base is built, industrialists can launch into exporting, especially when the domestic market is saturated. Government support for export promotion should include information about foreign markets, organizing trade fairs and, most importantly, quality control. The latter could be achieved by ensuring that protection does not eliminate domestic competitive pressures. Another pre-requisite would be putting the appropriate institutional mechanisms into place. (pp. 361–363).

The specific institutional mechanisms varied by country with South Korea using large conglomerates as did Japan to lead the process. South Korea licensed foreign technology and bought technical assistance but relied on domestic production. Japan relied more heavily on a consultation process with business leaders. In Taiwan public enterprises, often in partnership with multinational companies, drove the process of pushing imbalances and using incentives to induce "big push" responses from a large numbers of downstream firms. (p. 368) [refer to Chapter 2].

In the early stage of building a manufacturing base, capital controls are needed to curb speculative activity that could inflate the exchange rate with inflows or cause an investment collapse with an outflow. (p. 367). After export success has been attained, a gradual liberalization of imports can be put into place (p. 368). The whole process needs to be guided by a pilot agency, with meritocratic staffing and a great deal of operational flexibility. Ideally, strategic plans should only pertain to a few industries at a time (p. 371).

Ha-Joon Chang

Another strand in the developmentalist literature is that not only were the design principles outlined above prominent in East Asian catch-up development but that these principles were remarkably similar to those used by the currently advanced economies for their catch-up growth. The most prominent in such scholarship is Ha-Joon Chang's *Kicking Away the Ladder* (2002).[25] Chang points out that all currently advanced economies (with the exceptions of the Netherlands and Switzerland who were already close to the technology frontier) used extensive industrial, trade, and technology policies for catch-up growth.

Based on his historical analysis, Chang documents the various policies and tools used in the currently advanced economies that included tariffs, trade subsidies, duty drawbacks on inputs for exported goods, duty exemptions on imported equipment, industrial subsidies, public investment for infrastructure and manufacturing, and support for foreign technology acquisition, both legal (study tours, exhibition, and apprenticeships) and illegal (industrial espionage, skilled worker poaching, smuggling and patent infringement). Their focus was on building an indigenous technological capacity and so apart from the above modes of technology acquisition there was public support for acquisition of machinery for reverse engineering, diffusion of information, R&D, competitions and prizes for machine construction, formation of industry associations, procurement, quality control to protect national exporter reputation, research institute formation, education, and training. In addition, there were public-private ventures, directed credit, cartel formation, and deferment of monopoly rights to aid industrialization (pp. 22, 65). Policies and tools varied by country depending on history and institutional evolution, but Chang notes the uncanny resemblance of these methods with the industrial, trade, and technology policies adopted by the East Asian economies (p. 22).

Citing Friedrich List (1916, p. 4), who he points out was converted to protectionism after visiting the USA and studying the writings of Alexander Hamilton (1935), the first Secretary of the Treasury, he argues that blocking the use of the policies mentioned above amounts to "kicking away the ladder" that they utilized to attain prosperity. By documenting historical evidence on the use of industrial, trade and technology policies by the currently advanced economies, he seeks to verify one of his key hypotheses i.e. that the rich countries did not get rich by following liberal policies embodied in WTO rules and the structural adjustment policies of the World Bank and the IMF (p. 4). He cites evidence to demonstrate that the USA, which has been the chief advocate of liberal policies since the 1980s, was the most intensely protectionist country in the world between 1816 and 1945 (p. 61).

The debate on developmentalism

A debate on developmentalist thinking was triggered by the publication of *The East Asian Miracle: Economic Growth and Public Policy* (1993) by the World Bank. This study was commissioned by Japan as a prominent World Bank share-holder to explore alternative interventionist development policy prescriptions utilized in the growth of the East Asian economies. The foreword (iii–iv), signed by Lewis T. Preston, captures well the message the World Bank wanted to convey and this is echoed in the rest of the book.

First, the book expresses that the cause of East Asian (including Japan, South Korea, Taiwan, Singapore, Hong Kong, Indonesia, Malaysia, and Thailand) growth was "superior accumulation of physical and human capital" premised on high saving and investment. Second, these economies demonstrated a better allocation of resources than other development countries. These cover the classi-cal and neo-classical explanations respectively. Third, these countries ensured macroeconomic stability. Lastly, the book gives a nod to developmentalist think-ing in noting the ability of these East Asian countries to "acquire and master" technology.

The foreword conceded that some selective interventions improved market performance because they were implemented by able governments with a capa-city to enforce and monitor performance criteria. But it concluded that, in view of the challenging context and institutional requirements of getting intervention right, only the market oriented aspects of their policies could be recommended with few reservations. The rest of the book repeated these messages and pointed out variations in strategy. In addition, it noted that these East Asian economies benefited from declines in fertility that accompanied educational attainment, from limited price distortions relative to world prices (in comparison to the dis-tortions in other developing countries), and from encouraging manufactured exports, which forced producers to use best practice technology.

The World Bank contends that there are competing policy explanations for East Asian success (pp. 81–86). The neo-classical explanation summarized by "getting prices right" and the "revisionist" (developmentalist) explanation com-prised the views of Johnson, Amsden and Wade. As an alternative to these two views, the World Bank proffers a centrist and pragmatic market-friendly view premised on "getting policies right." This means first securing the macro-economic fundamentals. Following that, the right policies include limited price distortions, market competition, openness to trade, technology, foreign invest-ment, partnership, and open channels of communication with businesses, invest-ing in human capital, limiting inequality, and selective interventions that produce market conforming results.

This story is admittedly a far cry from the conventional neo-liberal story of "getting prices right," liberalizing, deregulating, and privatizing. However, it is also very different from the developpomentalist approach of "getting the prices wrong" with a technology and industrial policy based on protection, directed credit using development banks, and subsidies designed, in Wades' words, to

"lead the market". The World Bank argued that it would be difficult to disen-
tangle competing explanations and identify what exactly contributed to the economic growth, and the lack of counterfactuals makes certainty all the more
difficult.

Even so, the World Bank does seem to indicate considerable certainty with
regards to its own argument that only the market oriented aspects of policy can
be recommended with confidence, especially when the right institutions are not
in place. This provoked the ire of scholars including Dani Rodrik and Robert
Wade in *Miracle or Design* (eds. Fishlow *et. al*, 1994), which countered the
World Bank view.

Rodrik disputed that the East Asian economies conformed to good governance as indentified by the Bank (pp. 42–47). He identified the typical neo-
classical view of good governance as announcing simple and predictable rules
uniformly applied and honest bureaucrats who have arm's length relations with
businesses and limited discretionary powers to change these rules. Rodrik argued
that all these criteria were actually violated and that corruption was a noted
problem in all these countries. Also, what distinguished these economies were
not performance criteria per se as advocated by developmentalists, since other
developing countries also had them, but their ability to enforce them.

He also took issue with the World Bank's position that selective industrial
policy did not work. He argued that it is logically inconsistent to claim that the
tools were successful, but not the purpose for which they were used (p. 28). He
also challenged on methodological grounds the tests used to refute the effectiveness of selective industrial policy and the importance of export promotion
(pp. 31–42).

Like Rodrik, Wade also challenged the methodological grounds for the World
Bank's conclusions that selective industrial policy did not work, and that the
industrial structure that emerged was consistent with comparative advantage
rather than an outcome of industrial policy (pp. 57–69). Wade argued that industrial structure was predicted using per capita incomes of an average that included
highly interventionist countries and, furthermore, per capita income itself could
be a likely outcome of induced structural change based on selective industrial
policy. In addition, the results were likely to be sensitive to the time period
selected. He also challenged the inaccuracy of claims (non-promotion of textile
industries), one sided evaluations (focusing on the costs of heavy and chemical
industries in South Korea but not the benefits), and an inaccurate attribution of
failure to government bureaucrats.

Finally he demonstrated that the analytical framework (neo-classical economics) used by the World Bank was unable to capture the East Asian vision of
organizing and planning the development of their economies. This vision went
much beyond a simplistic "picking winners" that critics of industrial policy char-
acterize it as. Also, while the World Bank assumed that policy bifurcation was
possible, Wade argued that protection, export promotion, education, and industrial and technology policy were an integrated whole (pp. 69–74). Both (Rodrik
and Wade) commended the Bank for having addressed issues that the

mainstream normally ignored (i.e., the possibility that intervention could have worked) and both argued that the debate was far from resolved.

The extent to which the World Bank's thinking has changed by its critics is obvious when reading another landmark report, which it published in 2005: *Economic Growth in the 1990s: Learning from a Decade of Reform*. Once again, the foreword to the report contains its key messages, which are virtually identical to those contained in the *East Asian Miracle*: "Unquestionably it is macroeconomic stability, domestic liberalization, and openness that lie at the heart of any sustained growth process (p. xii)." The key functions of "accumulation of physical and human capital, efficiency in resource allocation, adoption of technology and sharing the fruits of growth (p. xiii)" still apply.

In this preface the World Bank seems to make no concession in maintaining that this standard neo-liberal approach will deliver growth. Also, further along it speculated that these conditionality driven structural reforms did not yield the expected growth because they were not sufficiently ambitious, or because of policy incoherence (conflicting conditionalities), or because of incorrect sequencing (p. 10).

However, it conceded there is more than one way to achieve growth and that the appropriate practices will depend on context or country specificities. Thus the Bank refuted the "one size fits all" conditionality embodied in structural adjustment loans. There is an acknowledgement that mere efficiency is not enough and that the developmentalist agenda of "structural transformation and diversification of production" is important. It conceded that various interventions and incentives, like duty rebate schemes and subsidized credit, might be effective (p. 12). Finally, it conceded that market failures needed to be addressed just as much as government failures did. (p. 10).[26] Ultimately, the difference between the two books is one of emphasis, although time will tell if the old policy conditionality has actually been replaced by flexibility and pragmatism that emphasizes industrialization, diversification, and building technological capacity rather than merely monetary and fiscal discipline and market driven efficiency.

Another issue is that the current incarnation of developmentalist option may no longer be a viable alternative given the altered global economic rules imposed by the WTO and international financial institutions. There is a debate on this issue of closing policy space. UNDP (2005, pp. 133–139) and Wade (2005) assume a pessimistic position on the availability of the developmentalist option. Chang and Grabel (2004, p. 69), Amsden (2005), UNCTAD (2006), Rodrik (2007), Chang (2009), and Cimoli, Dosi, and Stiglitz (2009, p. 555) assume an optimistic position about LICs still being able to finding creative ways of pursuing an industrial and technology policy.

Summary and conclusions

There are many commonalities in the narratives describing the spectacular growth of Japan, South Korea, and Taiwan. All of them seemed to follow the prescriptions of the early developmentalists in terms of the role of the state in engendering industrialization, even if they may not have been familiar with the writings of these scholars.

The "Japanese model," however, was certainly very familiar to South Korea and Taiwan, and it is not surprising that they drew on the basic design principles of the "Japanese model." The design principles of this model were summarized by Johnson (1982, pp. 315–320). They included a small, inexpensive but elite bureaucracy of mostly generalists with a very high level of managerial skill to conceive and execute industrial policy, as described in this chapter. These bureaucrats then needed to function in a political system where the legislature and judiciary created adequate space to "take initiative and operate effectively." A fine balance had to be maintained to ensure that intervention was "market conforming," ensuring adequate competition while preventing overcompetition and providing enough space for businesses to do what they do best.

Finally, the model required a pilot organization like MITI that had adequate powers to execute industrial policy. In Japan's case, the scope of MITI's authority extended to research, planning, energy, domestic production, international trade, and finance. These design principles were adapted to suit the historical and institutional conditions in South Korea and Taiwan.

However, in reading the path-breaking case studies that have contributed to the resurgence of developmentalism as an alternative, what stands out is that while the goal was the same (high speed or catch-up growth based on technological and industrial development) and there was broad similarity in methods, the specifics varied a great deal. An important theme in Johnson's work was showing how history, rather than culture per se, led to the evolution of social and economic institutions that were harnessed for high speed growth. This historical approach is echoed in the work of Amsden and Wade, and indeed Chang shows that current advanced economies used policies and tools very similar to the East Asian economies for their own catch-up growth but that the specifics depended on historical conditions and the relevant state of institutional evolution.

Another important commonality among new developmentalist authors is their view of development as a collective action issue that requires social consensus. Such a consensus, supported by norms of equality and inclusion, can create social tolerance for policies that might otherwise be considered high-handed and provoke a social reaction. In Japan's case, the common experience of poverty and hardship after the war and the broadly shared desire for catch-up enabled the economic bureaucracy to assume a leadership role in attaining this national goal. In South Korea's case, Amsden points out land reforms initiated by the Japanese colonizers for their own purpose but pushed much further to ensure "land to the tiller" by the US occupation forces (to match Soviet reforms in North Korea) ensured adequate food supply, dampened inflation and moved capital from land speculation into industry. Similarly, Wade points out that land reforms and agricultural support initiated by the Japanese in Taiwan but taken further by the Nationalists (mainlanders), along with blocking other avenues of wealth creation in finance put a premium on industrial wealth creation. Once again, social equality, wealth creation, and employment produced a social consensus

Amsden pointed out that the developmentalist model of late industrialization is based on "learning" rather than invention or innovation. An important precondition of this approach to development is reasonably good managerial ability to facilitate the learning for catch-up growth. However, once the catch-up has occurred, countries like Japan, Taiwan, and South Korea faced a new set of much steeper challenges as they moved beyond simply learning to begin innovating and inventing. The essence of developmentalism is to create the market and non-market conditions to enable continued learning, innovation, and diversification.

Notes

1 The introduction draws on Khan (2010) to frame the issues.
2 These terms are often used interchangeably. Refer to the introduction in chapter 2 for distinctions.
3 For definitions, refer to UNCTAD (2006, p. 196, fn. 2). For supportive expositions, refer to Amsden (2001), Wade (2004), Chang (2006), and Rodrik (2008). For a critique of industrial policy, refer to Pack and Saggi (2006) and to Chang (2009) for a commonality seeking rejoinder. The industrial policy debate between the World Banks's Justin Lin and Ha-Joon Chang (2009) is also important in this context. Lin apparently supports industrial policy but by arguing that it should be tied to comparative advantage effectively ridding it of the developmentalist prescriptive content. Baumol, Litan, and Schramm (2007, chapter 6) also assume a critical position but concede that state guided capitalism may be effective during the stage when low income countries borrow, adapt, and absorb technology ("imitate") but that they need to move beyond this to innovate, the ultimate diver of economic growth. For an extensive survey of the theory and broad evidence, refer to Harrison and Rodriguez-Clare (2009) who are skeptical that the available evidence or the tests conducted justify industrial policy on welfare grounds. For a left perspective on developmentalism, refer to eds. Fine, Sarasvati, and Tavasci (2011).
4 Critics charge that the state is unable to "pick winners" and that this should be left to the market. The "picking winners" critique may apply to HIC states trying to chart new territory such as clean energy.
5 Structural adjustment encompasses all aspects and sectors of the economy. Industrial policy is equally broad since its success is dependent on supportive sector policies.
6 Wade (2004) captures this well with his term "governing the market."
7 It would be a fair question to ask why the World Bank's endorsement matters. The answer is that the World Bank has been the most active producer and diffuser of economic development literature for several decades. Not all are impressed with the quality of the research or with the systematic ideological leaning of the policy advocacy it is used for (refer for example to eds. Bayliss, Fine, and Waeyenberge, 2011).
8 Khan (2009) distinguishes between "learning rents" and "redistributive rents" and success in industrial policy depends on the specific internal political economy that conditions the state's ability to manage rents to ensure learning and prevent mere acquisition.
9 Chang (2009) views exports as easy to monitor and preferable to internal performance criteria like profits which could be influenced by market power.
10 Without such competitive discipline, import-substitution industrialization can degenerate into crony capitalism, as was the case in many low income countries under ISI regimes.
11 In the foggy world of economic policy setting, no precision is implied in setting policy or in the ex ante knowledge of outcomes. Mistakes are expected and inevitable, but overall the states got it right.

12 The variant of structural adjustment programs called Poverty Reduction Growth Facility (PRGF), which continues to have the same debilitating "conditionalities" as earlier facilities, is hence viewed as an oxymoron. Structural adjustment has many critics for the poverty and inequality these programs are claimed to have resulted in. Among the most prominent from a feminist perspective is Elson (1992; 1995, chapter 8) who charged that advocates of these programs were unaware of the implicit male biases in structural adjustment programs. In fact, the negative impacts on women were much greater as the fiscal burden on the state was lightened and women had to work with tightening budgets to try to ensure service provision otherwise provided by the state. There was also blindness to women's reproductive role in economic models that treated labor as an abstract entity and also to the association of work within and outside the household whereby rising unemployment induced by structural adjustment required women to supplement dwindling household income and continue to bear the burden of household work unassisted by males.

13 I have presented their work chronologically and tried to minimize overlaps. In all cases my focus is on policies associated with "catch-up" growth.

14 While Johnson also considered and refuted other possible explanations for the Japanese miracle, the focus here is on his developmentalist story.

15 For Johnson, these were exceptions to MITI's remarkable success rate whereas for industrial policy opponents they represent examples suggesting that relying on the market is enough.

16 Gerschenkron (1962) is the classic Amsden often cites in this regard. He posited that the nature of catch-up growth and industrialization depended among other factors on the size of the gap and the unique institutional instruments/arrangements adopted sometimes as "substitutes" for what the leader countries possessed when developing. The ability of learning and acquiring from the leaders (technology/capital) was an advantage that the leader did not possess. Myrdal (1970, chapter 2) argues on the contrary that being a latecomer is a disadvantage due to the much more difficult initial conditions.

17 Amsden quotes Luedde-Neurath to indicate that even when trade was ostensibly liberalized, "the import regime remained restrictive and full of hidden obstacles" (p. 70).

18 In this context Amsden cites Kaldor (1967, 1978).

19 Heterodox economists question the existence of a free market since all markets and prices are institutionally determined, so it would in any case be difficult to know what free market prices are (Chang, H-J, 2010, pp. 1–10).

20 In a fuller and more general treatment of this issue in a later work, Amsden (2008, pp. 94–95) listed the state's objectives to include higher productivity and hence greater output and employment, a higher investment rate, improved management practices, local content, financial soundness, and R&D. In exchange, the state acquired popular support and higher tax revenues. She mentioned that performance criteria predated the discovery of conditionality by the Breton Woods institutions for their structural adjustment loans and that they represented an antidote to corruption (p. 98).

21 Chapter 6 provides a full account of how the developmentalist state engineered catch-up economic growth.

22 The focus in this chapter and book is on catch-up growth. Wade's update in the 2004 edition discussed post catch-up growth issues for Taiwan (pp. xxxvii–xli) as did Amsden (2003).

23 He discusses in detail differences of Taiwan's path with that of South Korea (pp. 320–325) and Japan (pp. 325–328).

24 Amsden (2008, p. 91) referred to import substitution as "the mother of exports."

25 Also notable is Reinhart (2007). They view the underlying vision of the developmentalist import substitution industrialization (ISI) program as incorrectly confuted

by a critical focus on the tools used by governments. This is much the same as associating the Marxist vision of social justice with the centralized high-handedness of the Soviet state.

26 These changes to the straight neo-liberal view have been referred to by Stiglitz (2008), World Bank Chief Economist 1997–2000, as the post-Washington Consensus.

References

Amsden, A. H. 2008. *Escape from Empire: The Developing World's Journey through Heaven and Hell.* Cambridge, Massachusetts: The MIT Press.

Amsden, A. H. 2005. "Promoting Industry under WTO Law." In: K. P. Gallagher, ed., *Putting Development First: The Importance of Policy Space in the WTO and Financial Institutions.* London: Zed Book.

Amsden, A. H. 2003, *Beyond Late Development: Taiwan's Upgrading Policies. Cambridge, Mass.*: The MIT Press.

Amsden, A. H. 2001. *The Rise of "The Rest": Challenges to the West from Late-Industrializing Economies.* Oxford: Oxford University Press.

Amsden, A. H. 1989. *Asia's Next Giant.* New York: Oxford University Press.

Baumol, W. J., Litan, R. E., and Schramm, C. J. 2007. *Good Capitalism, Bad Capitalism and the Economics of Growth and Prosperity.* New Haven: Yale University Press.

Bayliss, K., Fine, B., and Waeyenberge, E. V., eds., 2011. *The Political Economy of Development: The World Bank, Neoliberalism and Development Research.* New York: Pluto Press.

Chang, H.-J. 2010a. 23 *Things They Don't Tell You about Capitalism.* New York: Bloomsbury Press.

Chang, H.-J, 2010b, "Hamlet Without the Prince of Denmark: How Development Has Disappeared from Today's Development Discourse." In: Khan, S. R. and J. Christiansen, eds., *Market as Means Rather than Master: Towards New Developmentalism.* London: Routledge.

Chang, H.-J. 2009. "Industrial Policy: Can We Go Beyond an Unproductive Confrontation?" Plenary Paper for Annual World Bank Conference on Development Economic, Seoul, South Korea.

Chang, H.-J. 2006: *The East Asian Development Experience: The Miracle, the Crisis and the Future.* London/Penang: Zed Books/Third World Network.

Chang, H.-J. and Grabel, I. 2004. *Reclaiming Development: An Alternative Economic Policy Manual.* London: Zed Books.

Chang, H.-J. 2002. *Kicking Away the Ladder: Development Strategy in Historical Perspective.* London: Anthem Press.

Cimoli, M., Dosi, G., and Stiglitz, J. E. 2009. "The Future of Industrial Policies." In: M. Cimoli, G. Dosi, and J. E. Stiglitz., eds., *Industrial Policy and Development: The Political Economy of Capabilities Accumulation.* Oxford: Oxford University Press.

Elson, D. 1995. *Male Bias in the Development Process.* Manchester: Manchester University Press.

Elson, D. 1992. "From Survival Strategies to Transformation Strategies: Women's Needs and Structural Adjustment." In: L. Benería and S. Feldman, eds., *Unequal Burden: Economic Crisis, Persistent Poverty, and Women's Work.* Boulder: Westview Press.

Fine, B., Sarasvati, J., and Tavasci, D., eds., 2011. *Beyond the Developmentalist State.* London: Pluto.

Gerschenkron, A. 1962. *Economic Backwardness in Historical Perspective.* Cambridge, Mass.: Harvard University Press.

Hamilton, A. 1935. *The Reports of Alexander Hamilton on Public Credit, A National Bank, Manufacturers, and the Establishment of a Mint.* Washington, D.C.: Blair and Rives.

Harrison, A. and Rodriguez-Clare. 2009. "Trade, Foreign Investment, and Industrial Policy for Developing Countries." National Bureau of Economic Research Working Paper 15261, Cambridge, MA, www.nber.org/papers/w15261

Johnson, C. 1982. *MITI and the Japanese Miracle: The Growth of Industrial Policy, 1925–1975.* Stanford: Stanford University Press.

Kaldor, N. 1978. "Causes of the Slow Rate of Growth in the U.K." In *Essays in Economic Theory.* London: Duckworth.

Kaldor, N. 1967. *Strategic Factors in Economic Development.* Ithaca, N.Y.: Cornell University Press.

Khan, M. 2009. "The Political Economy of Industrial Policy." In: M. Cimoli, G. Dosi, and J. E. Stiglitz, eds., *Industrial Policy and Development: The Political Economy of Capabilities Accumulation.* Oxford: Oxford University Press.

Khan, S. R. 2010. "Towards New Developmentalism: Context, Program, Constraints." In: Khan, S. R. and Christiansen, J., eds., *Market as Means Rather than Master: Towards New Developmentalism.* London: Routledge.

Lin, J. and Chang, H.-J. 2009. "Should Industrial Policy in Developing Countries Conform to Comparative Advantage or Defy it? A Debate Between Justin Lin and Ha-Joon Chang." *Development Policy Review,* 27 (5), 483–502.

List, F. 1916. *The National System of Political Economy* (translated by Sampson S. Lloyd). New York: Longmans, Green and Company.

Myrdal, G. 1970. *The Challenge of World Poverty: A World Anti-Poverty Program in Outline.* New York: Pantheon Books.

Pack, H., and Saggi, K. 2006. "Is There a Case for Industrial Policy? A Critical Survey." *The World Bank Research Observer,* 21(2), 267–97.

Reinert, E. 2007. *How the Rich Countries Got Rich and Why Poor Countries Stay Poor.* New York: Carroll and Graf.

Rodrik, D. 2008. "Industrial Policy: Don't Ask Why, Ask How." *Middle East Development Journal* (Demo Issue), 1–29.

Rodrik, D. 2007. *One Economics Many Recipes: Globalization, Institutions, and Economic Growth.* Princeton: Princeton University Press.

Rodrik, D. 1994. "King Kong Meets Godzilla: The World Bank and the East Asian Miracle." In A. Fishlow *et al.,* eds., *Miracle or Design? Lessons from the East Asian Experience.* Washington D.C.: Overseas Development Council, Policy Essay No. 11.

Stiglitz, J. E. 2008. "Is there a Post-Washington Consensus." In: N. Serra and J. E. Stiglitz, eds., *The Washington Consensus Reconsidered: Towards a New Global Governance.* New York: Oxford University Press.

UNCTAD (United Nations Conference on Trade and Development). 2006. *Trade and Development Report.* New York: United Nations.

UNDP (United Nation Development Program). 2005. *International Cooperation at a Crossroads: Aid, Trade and Security in an Unequal World; Human Development Report 2005.* New York: Oxford University Press.

Wade. R. H. 2005. "What Strategies Are Viable for Developing Countries Today? The World Trade Organization and the Shrinking of 'Development Space.'" In: Gallagher, K. P. 2005. *Putting Development First: The Importance of Policy Space in the WTO and Financial Institutions.* London: Zed Book.

Wade, R. H. 2004. *Governing the Market: Economic Theory and the Role of Government in East Asian Industrialization.* Princeton: Princeton University Press.

Wade, R. H. 1996. "Japan, The World Bank and the Art of Paradigm Maintenance: The East Asian Miracle in Political Perspective." *New Left Review*, 217 (May/June), 3–36.

Wade, R. H. 1994. "Selective Industrial Policies in East Asia: Is the East Asian Miracle Right?" In: A. Fishlow *et al.*, *Miracle or Design? Lessons from the East Asian Experience*. Washington D.C.: Overseas Development Council, Policy Essay No. 11.

World Bank. 2005. *Economic Growth in the 1990s: Learning from a Decade of Reform*. Washington, D.C.: World Bank.

World Bank. 1993. *The East Asian Miracle: Economic Growth and Public Policy*. New York: Oxford University Press.

8 Reflections

While this book has reviewed the big thinkers in macro development economics, much of the current ferment and excitement in the field is in micro development economics. Abhijit Banerjee and Esther Duflo have spawned an industry of randomized evaluations and impact assessments.[1] Such evaluations also lend themselves easily to Ph.D. dissertations, enabling graduate students in economics to demonstrate both theoretical innovation and empirical skills.

The broad agenda driving their project is to find out what works to guide policy and also to make aid more effective for poverty alleviation. But, while one could argue that poverty alleviation, meeting basic human needs or supporting human development (see Chapter 5) serve as uniting motives, there is no stated overarching conceptual framework that seems to drive the randomized evaluation research project.[2]

That said, Rodrik finds in this project a mechanism to unify the micro and macro branches of development economics.[3] Along with other colleagues (2008), he has been at the forefront of elaborating on "growth diagnostics" to identify binding constraints for economies and in a flexible manner moving from one constraint to the next as the earlier problem is addressed and others become more pressing.[4] Both projects (randomized evaluation and growth diagnostics) share the commonality of troubleshooting and are ideally suited for a technical approach to economics. Growth diagnostics are perhaps less apt to spawn so many Ph.D. dissertations, given that there is a limited number of countries to study. While there have been a large number of case studies, so far this tool seems not to have captured the imagination of fresh entrants into the profession to the extent that impact assessments have.

Perhaps this focus on the margin or the small compared to the "big" thinking of the pioneers was inevitable. Take-off or catch-up growth has occurred in many countries and there is a sense of hope that others can follow and a greater confidence is evident in many LICs/MICs. The acrimonious North-South debates, while not irrelevant, are hence not as pressing as they were half a century ago (see Chapters 3 and 4). Graduate economics departments selecting on those with mathematical and quantitative skills may be weeding out those who have a comparative advantage in social thinking. Perhaps social thinking is subversive and paradigms have sentinels guarding them. Perhaps there is only so much economic intuition to go around and technicians are easier to produce and of more service in the academic industry.

Acemoglu and Robinson's *The Origins of Power, Prosperity, and Poverty* (2012) represents a refreshing change in this regard by attempting to explain why some countries succeed and most fail. Their political and economic history of the world addresses the big questions and one can only hope their work inspires young scholars in the economics profession. Their simple and powerful thesis has several aspects that I will dwell on at some length since doing so serves me well in concluding this book.

Acemoglu and Robinson view elites as universally prone to predation and self-enrichment. However, development is premised on harnessing the productive potential of much of the nation's population and hence requires inclusive political and economic institutions. Inclusive political institutions evolve historically via different mechanisms and processes in different countries (see North, Chapter 5). At critical junctures small differences can have lasting impacts due to cumulative causation and the onset of vicious and virtuous circles (refer to Myrdal, Chapter 4). Thus the Black Plague that decimated the population of England and Western Europe strengthened the hand of the peasantry that bid for higher wages (refer to Emmanuel, Chapter 3).

In England's case, this strengthened the hand of peasants who were providing free labor to oppressive feudal lords. Labor was able to bid for higher wages despite the monarchy's attempts to restore the old wages and forced labor. By contrast, in Eastern Europe the feudal lords were stronger and more predatory and even more ferocious, and feudal oppression emerged to repress the peasantry in what was called "the second serfdom." This difference was enough in leading to a very different historical evolution of institutions and economic growth trajectories.

A tradition of resistance was established in England, which was the first to fight for inclusive political institutions and associated economic freedoms. The Civil War of 1642–1651 and the Glorious Revolution of 1688 limited the power of the king and strengthened Parliament. Subsequently, the monarch had to negotiate to be given tax authority by Parliament and conceded more freedoms in exchange. In addition to reducing the monarchy's arbitrary authority over matters such as taxation, the British also achieved economic freedoms such as the granting of patents and other property rights, and the abolition of monopolies. The establishment of law and order further promoted commerce, and the monarch helped to promote industry, including by providing infrastructure.

These institutional changes promoting inclusivity set the stage for harnessing scientific breakthroughs for an industrial revolution. Since Parliament won the battle with the Monarch regarding the monopolization of trade, the merchant traders were enriched and used their capital accumulation for industrialization. The unlikely defeat of the Spanish Armada by England is an example of a fortuitous circumstance of great historical significance when the right circumstances and institutions are in place. In this case, it opened up the Atlantic merchant trading to the English and further strengthened the hand of Parliament to hold the Monarchy in check. The French and Spanish equivalents to the British Parliament lost this struggle and this consolidated England's lead.

The impact of the industrial revolution had differentiated impacts depending on the institutional evolution in the different parts of the world. There was institutional convergence via different paths and processes in Western Europe and the settler colonies of North America and Oceana and these regions were receptive to the diffusion of the industrial revolution. Eastern Europe had adopted an alternative path that had entrenched extractive institutions and was not receptive ground for such changes. Virtuous circles came into play in Western European countries as inclusive political institutions secured economic freedoms that harnessed the productive potential of most of the populations and economic growth and prosperity also strengthened political development.

The rest of the world was mired in vicious circles. Predatory institutions enriched only the elites who resisted technological changes that usher in creative destruction and more widespread prosperity and hence threaten their power and privileges. They only adopted military technological changes as instruments of repression. If there was growth, it was based on coercion, but since the latter did not tap the productive potential of the bulk of the population and resisted progressive changes in technology and political development, economic growth was not sustainable. England and other Western European nations did not spread inclusive political and economic institutions to the other regions and nations that they colonized since their interest was only in using these colonies to enrich themselves.

One lesson from this remarkable book is that political and social revolutions can change the economic trajectory of nations if inclusive political and economic institutions emerge from them.[5] The Arab Spring indicates the immense resistance existing political, administrative, and military elites mount to protect their privileges. In Egypt's case, subterfuge was used to diffuse the social mobilization and then via rearguard action the military reasserted the old order in the unfolding drama that is far from over. It seems that dictators become symbols of repressive regimes and removing them becomes confused with the more difficult goal of changing the predatory system. A social revolution in this regard is a terrible thing to waste given the enormous cost in terms of the loss of life and well-being and so the need for a focus and insistence on attaining the right objective.

Another lesson of this book is that nothing can be taken for granted and inclusive institutions can be rolled back after decades or even centuries. For example, in the USA elite education and political power are increasingly being monopolized by the very wealthy. The financial concentration at the turn of the twenty first century echoes the industrial concentration of the robber baron period of the late nineteenth century. These trends have created income inequality and marginalized talent, and this can foster political instability and undermine economic growth. The political system is still robust and saw push back in the form of the "occupy" movement. The emergence of political mobilizations can reverse destructive trends.[6]

Overall, this book provides a provocative and compelling thesis and the real strength of Acemoglu and Robinson's approach is not only in indicating how development occurred where it did but, more importantly, in explaining why it occurred first where it did. However, important questions remained unanswered about how catch-up growth actually happens and it is possible to proffer competing explanations for why it happens. Moreover, this thesis seems overly pessimistic for poor countries that are mired in a vicious circle with no apparent mechanism for a release. The underlying assumption of an inevitable proclivity to predation among leaders is contradicted by many counterexamples within the book and others in East Asia.[7] Finally, fitting East Asia into the same mold as Europe for explaining progress as they do seems to force the thesis and is not persuasive. In fact, the experience of East Asia points to a different explanation for progress and one that is more hopeful for currently poor countries.

While inclusive political and economic institutions may have emerged as part of the East Asian story, this happened after and not before catch-up growth occurred. What set off the process of growth was a sense of nationhood, possibly under siege, and the patriotic urge to do better and be ranked among the richer nations. As documented in Chapter 7 of this book, even dictatorial regimes can put a whole host of industrial and associated policies into place to achieve catch-up growth. Indeed, as indicated in Chapter 7, such interventionist policies were important mechanisms for how the currently rich countries got rich.

The really important and pressing issue is whether poor countries have simply missed the historical boat and need now await critical junctures such that small differences lead to favorable outcomes. There is far too much of a sense of urgency among poor countries for many of them to wait for the long span of history to unfold and the East Asian example has inspired catch-up growth among several such as Thailand, Malaysia, and Indonesia.

Unfortunately, colonial history has dealt many of them a bad hand[8] and multifarious ethnicities or nations wrapped into one are subject to tensions and strife rather than a sense of nationhood.[9] In such cases, institutional change and economic growth will have to await the forging of a national identity; shared historical experience, media, sports, and education can be used to accelerate this process. Poor nations with many ethnicities also confront a competition for resources that leads to real and imagined ethnic injustices, undermines the effort to create a sense of nationhood, and delays the emergence of collective action for catch-up growth. Centripetal forces forging homogenization and nationhood compete with centrifugal forces of poverty and ethnic strife. In this race against time, good policies that encourage inclusion can be an antidote to rifts bred by poverty.[10]

While a sense of nationhood may serve to promote catch-up growth and eradicate poverty, the irony is that nationhood is quickly becoming an outmoded concept for the other related key challenges facing humanity. As many scientists and social thinkers have pointed out, the world has reached an impasse the like of which has never been witnessed before. We are experiencing climate events of a scale, intensity, and impact that make the quest for catch-up growth illusionary. The impasse is that those that have passed the threshold into a high mass consumption society are resisting changing the life that they have become accustomed to. The rest are resisting any constraints on catch-up growth.

The key themes identified in this book are capital accumulation for classical economics, efficient resource allocation for neo-classical economics, and building endogenous technological capacity, diversifying, and moving up the industrial value chain for the developmentalists. However, the one key commonality among writers in this book is the recognition of the importance of knowledge, information, or technology, as variously phrased, no matter the paradigm or the approach within the paradigm that the authors advocated.

Technology is also touted as a way of getting out of the current climate change impasse. Such technology optimism may not be warranted given the rapid pace of climate change without global collective action. Relying on collective action within nation states for catch-up growth can undermine global collective action. Finding a way out of these conundrums poses a continuing challenge for "big" thinkers.

Many thinkers have noted the adage that, as far as promoting sustainable livelihoods, providing fish is less desirable than teaching how to fish—or better still, teaching how to make a net is preferable to providing a net. Building capacity for manufacturing fishing boats and then trawlers is even better. This thinking is reflected mostly at the micro level, say for participatory development (see Chapter 5), but not at the level of the nation state. For example, aid has been more about providing food but less about how to grow food better.[11] Growing food better is terrain that seems to be marked out for corporate agriculture just as multinationals guard turf regarding production technologies in manufacturing.[12]

As indicated in Chapter 7, throughout history nations have learnt and prospered, despite the lack of real assistance and despite the barriers set up, through whatever means they could muster. Those wanting to help need to reflect on the old adage mentioned above but applied to the macro level in the context of the following question: What is it that truly makes nations prosperous and independent? As earlier mentioned, an important recurring theme in this book is that what really counts is the ability of nations to develop and sustain an indigenous technological capacity. Given climate change, this must now be clean technology. How to help in this regard is the challenge for those who truly want to help nations in their efforts to develop. Those who are keen to address climate change have the opportunity to shape this process so nations avoid past mistakes of current HICs. Eventually, it is a community of strong nations that will bring together the world by making the concept of nation redundant.

In development economics, as in economics more broadly, the debate can be reduced to one between liberty and community.[13] Those fearful of the great socialist experiment or worst still, the impulses in Nazi Germany, resist collective action. The broadest manifestations of collective action are taxation and public service delivery by governments. In the USA, the historical resistance to collective action may go back to the war of independence and the philosophy of the "rugged individual" cherishing liberty.

Economists like Peter Bauer (Chapter 6) write passionately and with much logic and evidence supporting arguments. While all evidence in the social sciences can always be questioned, libertarian thinkers are caricatured when viewed as driven merely by an impulse to support the status quo from which the rich have the most to gain. They believe in incentives and efficiency and they believe these to be thwarted by public action intended to deliver good social outcomes.

One view of those writing in support of collective action in its various manifestations, with democratic safeguards for individual rights, is that this represents a move to a more compassionate and hence more advanced civilization. Those holding this view have more patience with making collective action more effective to attain equality of opportunity or alternatively to end all forms of exploitation. These debates are unlikely to end soon.

Notes

1 In Banerjee and Duflo (2011), written for the general reader, they draw on findings from many such studies.
2 Deaton (2010), Rodrik (2010), and Ravallion (2012) among others are not persuaded about the possibility of generalizing from these random control trials or even about such studies adequately addressing the selectivity problem, their alleged methodological strength. Another possible concern, among several raised by these authors, is the ethics of denying a beneficial intervention to the control group extended to the treatment group.
3 Talk on "Diagnostics before Prescription," Williams College, Center for Development Economics, Fiftieth Anniversary Conference, October 14, 2010.
4 For a critique, refer to Dixit (2007).
5 In contrast to this broad vision, Abhijit and Duflo (2011) make the case for small changes based on rigorous research that amount to "a quiet revolution." These could include small services like banking subsidies for the poor, bed nets and deworming, incentives for appropriate behavioral responses, better communications strategies to provide important information, and village audits and community participation for more transparency, accountability, diligence, and inclusion.
6 The "Tea Party Movement" was another such mobilization in recent US history. While I did not agree with the politics or the timing of its demands for fiscal responsibility, this movement seems to have skillfully converted grassroots support into political advantage because unlike the occupy movement it did not reject the mainstream political process.
7 Examples of nationally motivated enlightened leadership mentioned in the book include Okubo Toshimichi and Shimazu Hisamitsu of Japan, Quett Masire and Seretse Khama of Botswana, the two Roosevelts of the USA, Deng Xiaoping in China, and Luiz Inácia Lula of Brazil.
8 Refer to Amin (Chapter 3) and Frank (Chapter 4) and for contrary views Rustow (Chapter 2) and Bauer (Chapter 6).
9 Some ethnic groups like the Kurds, Palestinians, and Kashmiris have a highly developed sense of nationhood but not the land or political freedom within which to exercise catch-up growth. Myrdal (1956, p. 3) was concerned about integration and how development would facilitate national integration in underdeveloped countries and how this would facilitate international integration. Almost six decades later, this remains a critical issue for many LICs.
10 Economic globalization is another challenge faced by LICs where capital often has a triple advantage relative to labor. Capital owners start with an advantage and this leverage is enhanced because it is more mobile than labor. It gains a third advantage if LICs need balance of payment assistance and are required to engage in structural reforms (refer to Chapter 6). While some structural reforms are sensible for long term

growth others such as labor market reforms and deregulations strengthen capital further at the expense of labor and other social groups and the environment. Inclusive growth would require taking into account this inherent strength of capital to create a balance.

11 The alignment of interest of MNCs and national governments in what came to be called the "Green Revolution" was an exception. Notwithstanding the social and environment shortcomings of this technological diffusion, that became evident with time, it initially did much for food production (refer to Agarwal, Chapter 5). However, nations remained dependent on MNCs for the inputs and that was of course the incentive for the MNCs. The "bio-technology revolution" promoting sales of genetically modified seeds is definitely not about sharing technology.

12 Trade Related Intellectual Property Rights is one mechanism for doing this (refer to Chapter 7 on shrinking policy space for development).

13 This juxtaposition between liberty and community was made by N. Gregory Mankiw, "Politics Aside, A Common Bond for Two Economists," *New York Times* June 29, 2013, www.nytimes.com/2013/06/30/business/politics-aside-a-common-bond-for-two-economists.html

References

Acemoglu, D. and J. A. Robinson. 2012. *The Origins of Power, Prosperity, and Poverty: Why Nations Fail.* New York: Crown Business.

Banerjee, A. V. and E. Duflo. 2011. *Poor Economics: A Radical Rethinking About the Way to Fight Global Poverty.* New York: Public Affairs.

Deaton, A. 2010. "Instruments, Randomization, and Learning about Development." *Journal of Economic Literature*, XLVIII (2), 424–455.

Dixit, A. 2007. "Evaluating Recipes for Development Success." *The World Bank Research Observer*, 22 (2), 131–157.

Hausmann, R., Rodrik, D., and Velasco, A. 2008. "Growth Diagnostics." In: N. Serra and J. E. Stiglitz, eds., *The Washington Consensus Reconsidered: Towards a New Global Governance.* New York: Oxford University Press.

Myrdal, G. 1956. *An International Economy.* New York: Harper & Brothers Publishers.

Ravillion, M. 2012. "Fighting Poverty one Experiment at a Time: A Review of Abhijit Bannerjee and Esther Duflo's *Poor Economics: A Radical Rethinking of the Way to Fight Global Poverty.*" *Journal of Economic Literature*, L (1), 115–127.

Rodrik, D. 2010. "Diagnostics before Prescription." *Journal of Economic Perspectives*, 24 (3), 33–44.

Index

Acemoglu, D. 133–5
Agarwal, Bina 83, 84, 89, 91n21
agency, Sen's concept of 89
aggregate demand 36n8; developmentalists and 20
agrarian reform, Baran and 51
agricultural modernization, women and 83
agriculture: in developmentalist thought 31; eco-friendly 86; gender and 89; labor intensive, ILO and 88; OECD study and 100–1; relationship with industry 118–19; Ricardo and 6; Rostow and 31; small farmer 78–9
Amin, Samir 45–7, 53, 68
Amsden, Alice 111, 114–18, 126–7, 128n20
appropriate technology 86
Asia's Next Giant (Amsden) 114
Avineri, S. 8, 9, 14n12, 14n15

backwash effects 62–3
balanced growth: Hirschman and 23–4; Lewis and 25; Nurkse and 22
Banerjee, Abhijit 132
Baran, Paul 39–42; contributions of 50
barter economies, transition to market economies 77
basic human needs 54n1; Baran's concept of 40, 54n1
Basic Human Needs approach 78–9, 88, 91n8; defined 78
Bauer, Peter T. 87–8, 98–100, 103, 103n2, 104n4, 136
Bettelheim, Charles 54n6
"Big Push" 32–3; Rosenstein-Rodan's theory and 22
Boserup, Esther 83, 89
Brazil, Furtado's class analysis and 51
Brazilian Model of Development 43

Brundtland, Gro Harkem 87

capabilities, Sen's concept of 80–1
capital: natural 86; Smith and 3
capital accumulation 36n8; Bauer and Yamey and 104n4; in classical economics 11–12, 136; Furtado and 42; Hodgskin and 8; Lewis and 28; Malthus and 5; Marx and 39; Mill and 7; Nurkse and 22–3; Ricardo and 6, 12
capital labor ratio, Ricardo and 6
capitalism: Baran and 51; evolution of, Baran and 40; Frank and 64–5; Marx and 39; Marxian analysis of 8; structuralism and 63–4, 68; Warren and 47–50, 53
Cardoso, Fernando Henrique 65–6, 68
case study research 110
center-periphery concept 57–8, 67
chaebols 115
Chambers, Robert 81–2, 89
Chang, Ha-Joon 111, 122–3, 126
Chilean development, *versus* Taiwanese 117
China, infrastructure investment in 80
circular cumulative causation, Myrdal's theory of 61–2, 68, 69n15
civil liberties: growth and 80; Sen's concept of 89
class: Amin and 45–6; Baran and 41; Marx's theory of 39
classical economic theory, contemporary relevance of 1–2
classical political economics, radical 7–11
classicial economic theory, key thinkers in 2–13
clean energy, financing of 86
collective action, controversy over 136–7
colonialism: Baran and 40, 50; Bauer and

For Product Safety Concerns and Information please contact our EU
representative GPSR@taylorandfrancis.com
Taylor & Francis Verlag GmbH, Kaufingerstraße 24, 80331 München, Germany

www.ingramcontent.com/pod-product-compliance
Ingram Content Group UK Ltd.
Pitfield, Milton Keynes, MK11 3LW, UK
UKHW020947180425
457613UK00019B/575

9 780367 866495